Hercules

The First Superhero
(An unauthorized biography)

Philip Matyszak

Monashee Mountain Publishing

Philip Matyszak has a doctorate in Roman history from St John's College, Oxford University and is the author of many books on Ancient History including the best-selling *The Greek and Roman Myths: A Guide to the Classical Stories,* *Ancient Rome of Five Denarii a Day* and *Legionary: The Roman Soldier's (Unofficial) Manual.* He teaches e-learning courses in ancient History for the Institute of Continuing Education at Cambridge University. For more information visit: www.matyszakbooks.com

First published in 2015 by Monashee Mountain Publishing (Canada)

ISBN 978-0-9881066-5-9

Cover illustration by Ravastra Design Studio

E-mail: info@ monasheemountainpublishing.com
Website: www.monasheemountainpublishing.com.

This book is dedicated to Clive Duncan

hip surgeon extraordinary,

and the staff at the G.F. Strong Rehabilitation Centre

who literally got me back on my feet.

Acknowledgements

Every book is a team project, and I would like to thank those who helped to prepare this book, including Adrian Goldsworthy and Jeremy Day who commented on the early drafts, and Christian Posratschnig and the community at UNRV who were involved with the project right from the start.

Even more thanks are due to my wife Malgosia who not only put up with a husband who went missing in ancient Greece for days on end, but even forgave me enough to provide invaluable help in editing the final text.

Contents

Foreword

I am not ignorant of the many difficulties facing those who attempt to relate the myths of antiquity, and nowhere is this more so than with the myths about Hercules. So great are the feats which he accomplished that everyone agrees on this: in all the legends that have been passed down from the memory of our earliest times, Hercules has surpassed all men. Consequently it is a challenge to give an account of such deeds in a manner which is worthy of them; to find powers of description which match labours so enormous that their very magnitude won the prize of immortality.

Also of course, these are stories from the dawn of time, and the details of each tale are so astonishing as to stretch belief. So the writer must either pick his facts, and edit away the most incredible achievements, or tell it like it was. The choice therefore is to either sully by omission the fame of the demi-god, or to sully his credibility by giving a full account.

The blame lies with those readers who demand of ancient legends the same degree of exactness and verisimilitude as for events of our own time. Using their own lives as a measure, these people doubt the possibility of feats as great as those of Hercules. They estimate his strength by the weakness of men today, and so find his acts unbelievable.

Generally speaking, it is unreasonable to examine the myths with a sceptical eye. In myth it is as with the theatre, where even if we are convinced there were no Centaurs with bodies of two different species, nor yet any Geryones with three bodies, we still look upon such productions with favour. By our applause we honour the god, and so should it be with myth.

Hercules, while still numbered among the mortals, managed through his own efforts to civilize the known world. Yet, oddly enough, people today forget the blessings which he has bestowed upon mankind, and instead they mock the praises heaped on him for his noblest deeds. ...

However, we shall leave such considerations aside. Instead I shall tell his story from the beginning, basing my tale upon those of the most ancient poets and writers of myth.

Diodorus of Sicily, writing around 2050 years ago. *History* 4.8ff

iii

Introduction

Hercules – everyone knows the name, but how many know the person? One of the most intriguing things about Hercules is that this mythical character is completely credible. Not Hercules the Superman, since even minds in the ancient world boggled at stories such as that of Hercules pulling the continents of Europe and Africa closer together just to make the Straits of Gibraltar a bit narrower.

However, Hercules the man is someone we can feel we know, even if we might not very much like what we discover about him. Even though he is a thief, a rapist and a murderer, Hercules does not think of himself as a bad person. Nor indeed was he, when judged by the very different standards of his day. Prickly, proud and with a tendency to use violence as a first resort, Hercules was a very dangerous man to be around. The casualty rate among his nearest and dearest easily surpasses that of a front-line combat regiment. Nevertheless, Hercules is an oddly sympathetic character.

Hercules never goes out of his way to be cruel, and sometimes he goes out of his way to be kind. Despite this, the Hercules of myth has certainly not the steely-eyes, square-jaw and morally flawless character of many modern superheroes. In fact, it is those very flaws that make Hercules interesting. Here is a man of limitless strength, born into a society which admires strength and sets very few moral limits on what a man can do with it. In those circumstances, how does the man who has slain so many monsters hold back from becoming a monster himself?

As we will see, Hercules at times teeters on the brink, but always pulls back from that last step, until eventually he does cross the line. He captures and pillages a city and then kills its king - all because that king objected to Hercules' plan to rape his daughter. There is poetic justice in the fact that this obnoxious deed led directly to the death of Hercules - though poetic justice is to be expected in a tale originally told by poets.

Today Hercules is defined purely by his famous Labours, which are seen as happening in isolation. This book re-integrates Hercules with the world of myth. We see him travel with Jason and the Argonauts in search of the Golden Fleece and meet the young King Priam, ruler of Troy.

The complete story of Hercules evolved over almost a millennium of myth-making. The legend existed for centuries before the first deeds were put into writing, and if there ever was a man on whom the original legend was based, his true identity is long lost in the mists of time. The tale has outgrown its origin.

In this book has drawn on sources as early as Homer's prehistoric Greece and as late as the last days of the Roman empire. As with any story told by a multitude of narrators over a period of time, there are discrepancies, chronological oddities and different points of view. In assembling this - one of the first complete biographies of Hercules in the the past two thousand years - my task has been less that of author than of editor. It has involved bringing together the different traditions, sorting them into a coherent chronology and above all, letting the ancient narrators speak with their own voices. (For this reason, my Greek translations are given with the hero's proper name, which was 'Heracles' and my Latin translations and the general text use 'Hercules'.)

My role has been to describe the social and political background to events, and explain why Gods and men acted as they did. To us, their deeds may seem vindictive, cruel and frighteningly arbitrary, yet in their own time and place these actions made perfect sense. This book attempts to take the reader to that time and place, and see the world of Hercules as Hercules himself saw it.

This is not a pleasant world. It contains much that is brutal and horrible. But it is also a world of wonder, where strange creatures roam, and Gods and men freely intermingle. There is a dryad in every tree, and a nymph in every pond. As you travel through this strange, beautiful and cruel landscape, you need not fear its denizens. You have Hercules by your side — and that is terrifying enough.

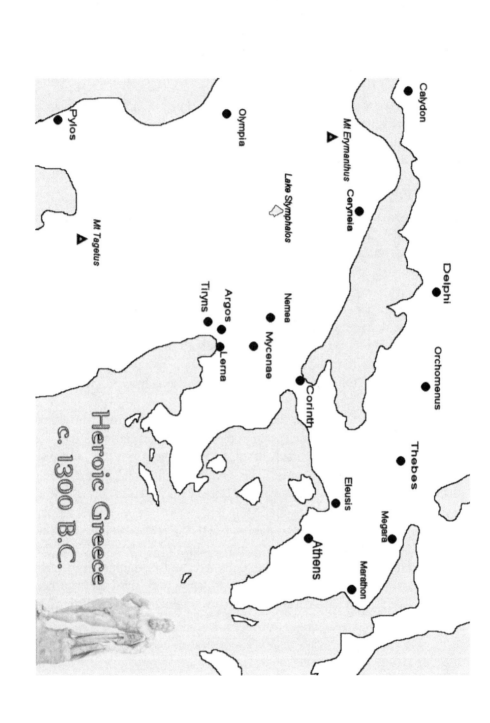

Heroic Greece
c. 1300 B.C.

Calydon

Pylos

Olympia

Mt Erymanthus

Ceryneia

Lake Stymphalos

Mt Tagetus

Delphi

Nemea

Tiryns

Argos

Lerna

Mycenae

Corinth

Orchomenus

Thebes

Eleusis

Megara

Athens

Marathon

Chapter 1

A noble ancestry, and a difficult birth

Our story begins with a maiden chained to a rock. Not any maiden, for in the nature of such stories the victim has to be a princess. The original legend is silent on the subject, but the fevered imaginations of later artists - such as Rembrandt and Titian - will demand that the princess be naked.

For this is not just any princess, but the famous Andromeda, princess of Aethiopia. Andromeda is beautiful, very beautiful, and this has proven her undoing. For the mother of Andromeda was very proud of her daughter's beauty, and proclaimed it to the skies. Had the mother stopped there, all would have been well, and Andromeda and her beauty would have passed unremarked by later generations. But the mother praised her daughter's beauty not just to the skies, but also to the seas.

More specifically, the proud mother boasted to the Ocean that her daughter was more beautiful than the Neriads, the sea-nymphs who were the daughters of Poseidon. Such beauty contests by proxy may be common enough among the parents of nubile daughters, but it is a dangerous game to play when one of the parents is the Lord of the Sea, a senior god with a proud and irritable disposition. Poseidon was insulted that his offspring might be considered inferior to mere mortals, and he proceeded to demonstrate why offending the God of tidal waves and earthquakes is a really bad idea.

Among the many strange creatures in Poseidon's watery domain was a monster called Cetus (which really means a monster called 'monster', since 'cetus' is what large sea creatures were called, and why whales today are 'cetaceans'). This particular Cetus was a sort of rampaging amphibian, almost as comfortable on the land as the sea. Following Poseidon's orders, Cetus started ravaging the coastline of Aethiopia.

Nowadays this would be a tricky task, since modern Ethiopia is completely land-locked, but the Aethiopia of myth was a larger place. The shoreline of the kingdom extended up the Mediterranean as far as the port of Joppa. Joppa is modern Jaffa, which as well as being famous for oranges, is also a port with a strong cetacean connection. Apart from being visited by Cetus, it is also from Joppa that (in a different tradition) the prophet Jonah later set out for his date with destiny inside a whale.

Cetus had a special motive for his trip to Joppa. To save what was left of his country, the king of Aethiopia had reached a deal with Poseidon. The agreement was that the monster would stop his ravages after one last act of violence. That last act would be to kill and devour Andromeda, who was to be delivered up for sacrifice, chained to a rock (with or without clothing, depending on one's artistic sensibilities). One can imagine a degree of terseness in the conversation between Andromeda and her parents as the latter stood beside the rock wringing their hands in anguish. But so still did Andromeda stand awaiting her fate that a passing hero almost mistook her for a statue, and indeed would have done so had her hair not stirred in a passing breeze.

This hero was Perseus, son of rich-haired Danae, and heir to the throne of Argos. Perseus was not really looking for another adventure at that point, for he had so recently slain the monstrous Medusa that her head was still bleeding from the bag he carried at his waist (the blood drops became the venomous snakes of Africa). However, no hero could overlook the monstrous shape of Cetus rising slowly from the deep, or ignore the shriek torn from Andromeda at the sight of her approaching doom.

Perseus could have passed on unseen, for at this point he was as invisible as the air beneath his feet. For Perseus still flew on the winged sandals he had borrowed from Hermes for his mission to slay Medusa, and he was also equipped with the helm of Hades which made him (and usually Death) completely invisible. However Perseus was not the only winged being in the skies around Joppa - and he was far from invisible to Eros. Unerringly nailed by one shot from the love-god's bow, Perseus fell hopelessly in love with the chained maiden. This left him with the options of either suffering through a remarkably brief and tragic romance or doing something drastic about Cetus, who was coming on fast.

For look! As a galley furrows the sea with its pointed prow when the rowers sweat and strain, so the breast of the monster rolls the waves aside.

Thus, as Cetus closed in on his helpless prey, the Roman poet Ovid takes up the tale in his *Metamorphoses*. There was no time to waste so - as any good Greek boy was obliged to do - Perseus quickly presented his case to the parents of his beloved. In about as many words Perseus told them, 'It's me or the monster, and frankly, if she takes me she could do much worse.' The frantic parents had barely time to agree, for Cetus was literally a stone's throw away.

He was now no further from the rock than Balearic slingers can hurl their flying missiles across the sky. But [Perseus] suddenly sprang from the ground and soared into the clouds. The monster saw his shadow on the sea and savaged what it saw.

Perseus swooped down through the air to the creature's back and sank his crescent blade deep into its shoulder. Sorely wounded, the beast roared, and reared upright, high in the air. Then it dived below the waves, then turned in frenzy like a fierce boar when the hunting pack bays all around.

Yet Perseus on his swift wings eludes the snapping jaws and plunges his curved sword between the ribs, into the monstrous back, all rough with barnacles, and anywhere vulnerable even to the tapering fish-tail end. The beast vomits sea spray and purple blood together, and so soaked are the ankle wings of the sandals of Perseus that he can trust them no longer. He sees a rock, exposed in the water, but awash in the turbulence. With his left hand braced on a ridge he steadies himself and stabs, over and over, at the monster's groin.

Ovid *Metamorphoses* 4.80ff

By some accounts it was Eros himself who freed Andromeda from her bonds, while Perseus hastily made himself presentable by scrubbing his blood-drenched body in a nearby stream. (Later Roman tourists paid good denarii to see that stream, which still ran red thanks to an algae bloom. They also came to see the Rock of Andromeda and the grooves which the chains had cut into it.)

3

Pursues v. Cetus with Andromeda in her usual state of artistic undress
Detail from an 18th century painting by Charles-Antoine Coypel now in the Louvre

Joppa is on a hill in front of which is a rock. On this rock they point out the marks made by the chains with which Andromeda was fastened.
Pliny the Elder, *Natural History* 5. 69

There was a bit of unpleasantness later, when the former fiancé of Andromeda violently objected to the sudden change of wedding plans. But Perseus literally petrified the man by showing him Medusa's head, which had lost none of its power for being severed. This rather mundane interruption aside (for it was not the first nor the last time that a former boyfriend would get stoned at a wedding) the path of true love ran smoothly for Andromeda and Perseus.

Perseus was indeed a prince, but once he returned home he never claimed his birthright to become king of Argos. Instead, while travelling in central Greece, he dropped his cap and found some mushrooms growing in the place where it fell. This place of the mushrooms ('Mycenae' in Greek) was so congenial a spot that Perseus founded a city there. In later years that city went on to become the greatest in Greece, and the children of Perseus became leaders and legends throughout the peninsula.

Perseus and Andromeda remain together even now; as constellations in the northern sky. Perseus still holds the head of Medusa, whose eye is now the star Agol ('the demon' in Arabic). Perhaps he does this to ward off the in-laws, for Andromeda's parents Cepheus and Cassiopeia have moved into nearby constellations. Poseidon did get his final revenge on Cassiopeia; for she is fixed in the night sky with her head towards the Pole Star. Thus as the stars wheel through the heavens, the boastful queen is fated to spend half of her nights upside-down.

Dynastic affairs

Millennia before the Montagues and Capulets, there were the Pelopids and the Perseids. Today the Perseids are best known as a meteorite shower that lights up the night sky in August. The meteorites appear to come from the direction of the constellation of Perseus, hence the name.

However in the heroic age of Greece, the Perseids were the children of Perseus, and a dominant force on the peninsula. That dominance was challenged by the accursed Pelopids. 'Accursed' here is literal fact rather than a casual pejorative. The patriarch of the Pelopid family was the infamous Tantalus. He, for reasons we need not go into here, once decided to feed the Gods a memorable meal. This meal was mainly his son Pelops, cut into sections and served with beans and a nice ambrosia. While the other gods abstained from the meal with horror, the corn goddess Demeter absent-mindedly ate a shoulder. (Hades had just kidnapped and raped her daughter Persephone, so Demeter was understandably distraught.) For this and other misdeeds, Tantalus was exiled to Tartarus - which was a sort of maximum security prison for cosmic undesirables - and tormented by having food and drink forever just outside his reach. It is from this punishment, and not from the meal he served the Gods, that we get the word 'tantalize'.

Pelops was restored to life, albeit with an ivory shoulder to replace Demeter's main course. In later life Pelops (his name means 'the dark one') courted Hippodamia, a relative of Perseus. To win his bride, Pelops also had to win over his prospective father-in-law. This father-in-law was King Oneomaus, himself a nasty character. He was in the habit of challenging his daughter's suitors to a chariot race and executing them when they lost. To make sure that he avoided this fate, Pelops removed several vital components which held together the chariot of Oneomaus, and replaced them with substitutes made of beeswax. Oneomaus perished in the subsequent race-day crash, but his charioteer survived. Even worse, the charioteer was aware of the cause of the crash, so Pelops threw him off a cliff to silence him. There were two consequences to this deed. On the positive side, Pelops won his race, won his bride and took over the now vacant throne of the kingdom. The successful race was commemorated in a regular sporting festival which was later expanded (by Hercules) to become the Olympic Games.

As a ruler Pelops was so effective that the land he ruled has ever since been called 'the Peloponnese'. The only obstacle to the complete Pelopid domination of the peninsula was Perseus, whom Pelops was unable to overcome. Pelops' efforts at domination were also hampered by the negative consequences of his victory. The charioteer whom Pelops had thrown off the cliff had cursed his killer all the way down.

The curse stuck, not just to Pelops but to his entire clan. Pelop's wife Hippodamia later hanged herself, and the family line was thereafter distinguished by fratricide, incest and cannibalism. The last generation wrapped up with Agamemnon - killed by his wife, but not before he had killed his daughter - and Electra and Orestes who killed their mother.

The star-crossed Pelopids are relevant to the story of Hercules because of a woman called Nicippe. Nicippe was born to Hippodamia in the years before her mother's suicide and she married a Perseid, a son of Andromeda and Perseus called Sthenelus. This marriage was one of a number of dynastic matches which took place when Perseids and Pelopids made love not war, and transferred their rivalry to the marriage bed.

Sthenelus, as might be expected of a prince of the Perseid line and ruler of a Mycenaean kingdom, had a busy and complex life. During his rule, he drove into exile a man called Amphitryon, who had killed Sthenelus' brother and was engaged to marry his niece, the fair Alcmene. Sthenelus did not know it, but by this action he set in motion a chain of events which was to transfer rivalry for the Mycenaean kingdoms from the Peloponnese to the heavens, and from the families of Perseus and Pelops to the family of the Olympian gods.

The birth of Hercules (and of Eurystheus)

Alcmene was superlative among women in form and beauty. None born of mortal woman in the bed of mortal man could compete with her in intellect, while her face and her dark eyes were as persuasive as the face and eyes of Aphrodite.
Hesiod *The Shield of Heracles* 1,1

So the poet describes the grand-daughter of Perseus, the betrothed of Amphitryon, and niece of Sthenelus. Given these attributes, it is little wonder that Amphitryon, the mighty spear-weilding warrior, was putty in his fiancée's hands. The love-struck swain was readily persuaded to make war on the people of Taphos. Alcmene had a justified grudge against this people, for they had slain her brothers. The Taphains dwelt in north-western Greece, and the war was long and complex enough to merit an epic of its own. (Which it got, though there is no space here for the stirring tale of battle, lust and treachery which kept Amphitryon from the arms of his beloved.) Suffice it to say that Amphitryon emerged triumphant from his war, and rushed home to celebrate his victory with the beautiful Alcmene.

Now, being a beautiful princess in the world of Heroic Greece had its hazards, and chief of these hazards was Zeus. Danae, the mother of Perseus and great-grandmother of Alcmene, had already discovered that being securely locked in a tower was no protection for the perpetually oversexed King of the Gods. Zeus was married to his sister, Hera, and so had few inhibitions about incest with his own descendants. Indeed, he is one of the few beings outside the *genus cuniculis* (rabbit family) who has managed to become his own great-uncle.

Alcmene, so the poet Hesiod tells us, was so devoted to her Amphitryon that she would look at no other man, nor indeed at any god, even Zeus himself. Zeus was well aware of this, and so began his seduction of Alcmene by turning himself into the form of Amphitryon. In this disguise he appeared as the beloved of Alcmene, home early from the wars and brandishing a Taphian cup as proof of his success.

What has been done there at the army ... [Zeus] is now relating to Alcmene. She, who actually is with a lover, thinks she is with her own husband. Zeus is

7

now relating how he routed the enemy host and took a fortune in booty. That
loot taken by Amphitryon has now been looted from him. What he wants, Zeus
easily gets.

Hermes in the prologue to *Amphitryon*, by the Roman playwright
Plautus.

The night which followed was indeed the stuff of myth, for it consisted of
multiple bouts of vigorous sex interspersed by long anecdotes in which
Zeus/Amphitryon recounted the doings of his *alter ego* in the wars. If it
seemed to Alcmene that the night of lovemaking and story-telling seemed to
last as long as three normal nights, that is because it did. Zeus was having far
too good a time to pack it in with the dawn, so he used his prerogative as King
of the Gods to extend the night until he - and presumably Alcmene - were well
and truly sated.

This unnaturally long night of epic sex had an unexpected side-effect. Not
only was Alcmene made pregnant, but the same egg was fertilized repeatedly
by the seed of Zeus. More divine essence and strength was transferred to the
newly-conceived child with each iteration, and Zeus realized that the result
would become someone exceptional even by the standards of his own
remarkable offspring.

Yet the reproductive process was not yet done with Alcmene. The very next
day Amphitryon came home from the wars and swept his beloved into bed
without further ado. The truth came out afterwards, possibly when Alcmene
commented either on her partner's different technique or enduring stamina.

By then it was too late. The son of Zeus now shared Alcmene's womb with
a son of Amphitryon, in a process known to modern gynaecology as hetero-
parental superfecundation. Even now, all might have been well, but Zeus was
so excited by the potential of the son he had just fathered that he failed to
keep his mouth shut. When the birth was due, Zeus announced that the
descendant of Perseus born that day would finally put the rivalry of the
Pelopids and Perseids aside and become the ruler of Mycenae and the
Peloponnese.

Enter Hera, Queen of the Gods, wife of Zeus, and the future bane of Hercules'
existence. Hera knew of, and bitterly resented her husband's numerous
infidelities. However, Zeus was the King of the Gods. He was also Hera's

husband, and he was therefore - gender discrimination in this era being as malignantly alive and well among Gods as it was with men - Hera's lord and master. Zeus was beyond punishment so, as one Roman writer explained, 'if you can't beat the donkey, you hit the saddle'. The frustrated Hera took out her venom at her husband's affairs on his paramours, however unwilling they had been, and punished their children, no matter how innocent.

This was a situation that would have been familiar to every ancient Greek and Roman who heard the story. As the later Roman writer Seneca says, 'To take a mistress is a grave offence to a wife'. (Letters 95.37) Everyone knew the injustice of punishing a slave girl for being raped by her master, but everyone knew it happened. To the Greeks and Romans the tragedy of Hera's victims was real life writ large, with princesses suffering in the same way as slaves.

Through no fault of their own, Alcmene and her unborn son had become the subject of the deadly vindictiveness of a powerful deity. Innocence neither excused them nor mitigated the punishment. Hercules and his mother were victims of circumstance, and when the Greeks and Romans followed the stories of Hercules' life, they did so mainly to see how he coped with those circumstances.

(It was the Graeco-Roman view of the world that no man was responsible for the hand that life dealt him, but the manner in which he played that hand gave the measure of the man.) Hera had decided that there was no way that Zeus' bastard son was going to become king of Mycenae and the Peloponnese. Since Zeus had already pronounced that the descendant of Perseus born that day would be king, this would happen. This would happen because Zeus was a Greek god, and Greek gods had integrity.

In the modern world, integrity is a good thing - a person says that he thinks, and does what he says. There is no disparity between his thoughts, words and actions. They are integral, which is what the word 'integrity' means. While integrity may be wonderful in a human being, when you are an all-powerful god, integrity is something of a curse. You have only to think a thing and, thanks to your divine power, it is done - and irreversibly done; because being a God not only means never having to say you're sorry, it also means not being able to undo your actions. (When you think about it, the universe would rapidly become a mess if the Gods started second-guessing themselves.) Integrity and the inability to go back and correct missteps do much to explain the notoriously poor impulse control of the Olympian Gods in myth.

In the case of Hercules, integrity meant that once Zeus had declared that the descendant of Perseus born that day would be king, the matter was set in stone. It would happen, no matter what. This left Hera with just two cards to play. One was the goddess Eileithyia, who, by some accounts was Hera's daughter. The other card was that Zeus had not specified which descendant of Perseus would be king. It will be recalled that the Pelopid Nicippe (p.6) had married a son of Perseus, and it so happened that at this time Nicippe was also pregnant, though only in her seventh month.

This is where the goddess Eileithyia came in, for Eileithyia was the Goddess of Childbirth. It was up to Eileithyia whether a birth was quick and easy, or prolonged and painful. She was 'Hera's daughter, who holds power over the bitter pangs of childbirth', as the poet Homer puts it. (Homer *Iliad* 11.270).

Once Hera had given her orders, it was the work of moments for Eileithyia to put the birth of Alcmene's child on hold, leaving the mother racked by the pains of a fruitless labour. While Alcmene suffered, Eileithyia sped to Mycenae and there induced Nicippe into a speedy and productive birth, for all that the child was two months premature. Thus was born Eurystheus, son of Nicippe and Sthenelus, grandson of Perseus and Andromeda, and king of Mycenae by birth and the word of Zeus. The other grandson, the son of Zeus, remained locked within the tortured womb of Alcmene - and could stay there forever as far as Hera and Eileithyia were concerned.

For seven days Alcmene sweated it out. She might have suffered longer were it not for her nurse. This nurse was Galinthias, a childhood friend of Alcmene and herself of semi-divine origin. Thanks to her supernatural origins, Galinthias was able to note the furtive presence of Eileithyia at the bedside, and quickly observed that the Goddess was there to hinder rather than help.

Another advantage of being semi-divine was that Galinthias was able to directly contact those mystic beings whom no mortal could approach. Leaving the bedside of her friend, Galinthias hurried through secret ways to the cave where the Fates span into the huge tapestry of life the threads which described the destiny of every living being. As expected, Galinthias found Clotho, the spinner, holding tight to the thread which waited to weave Alcmene's unborn son into the web of the world. Loudly, the nurse proclaimed that through the will of Zeus, a child had been born to Alcmene. So startled was Clotho by the announcement that she relaxed her grip on the thread. This immediately sprang into the web, irrevocably becoming part of the tapestry of life. Eileithyia had been sidestepped, and the child had been born - albeit a week too late to claim his inheritance.

The deception of Galinthias brought not one child into the world, but two. It will be remembered that Amphitryon had slept with Alcmene when he returned from the wars the day after Zeus had slept with Alcmene while pretending to be Amphitryon returned from the wars. Both sessions had been fruitful, so Amphitryon became the proud father of his own son, Iphicles, at the same time as he became the unwilling step-father of Zeus' offspring.

(Incidentally, so traumatized was Amphitryon by the whole business that he never slept with Alcmene again. Nor is this the only manner in which Alcmene became something of a terminus stop in sexual relations. Zeus thereafter never again slept with another mortal woman, claiming - rather ambiguously - that he had out-done himself with Alcmene.)

Hera had succeeded in her intent, for the descendant of Perseus born on the day of Zeus' rash announcement was Eurystheus, son of Nicippe. Eurystheus thus became the future king of Mycenae, usurping the son of Zeus from his predestined role. Nevertheless, Hera was by no means done with the child of her husband's adulterous union. To signal her continued malice, she brutally punished the nurse Galinthias for having allowed the child to be born at all. Galinthias was turned into a polecat, a creature ill-famed in antiquity for its incontinence and bizarre reproductive habits.

(Actually this revenge was something of a flop, because the witch-goddess Hecate had a soft spot for the underdog - or undergod - and she adopted the weasel/nurse into her retinue. This led to the creature being rehabilitated in the classical world, where many households adopted a pet weasel in Hecate's honour.)

As for the child himself, now that he had made his way into the world despite Hera's best efforts, the Queen of the Gods decided to get the brat out again; and as speedily as his arrival had been tardy. Galinthias' successor as nurse takes up the tale for an amazed Amphitryon;

Now shall I make you privy to matters even more wonderful. After the boy was laid in the cradle, two immense crested serpents glided down through the skylight. Instantly they both reared their heads ... and began to gaze all around. After they had located the children, they immediately headed for the cradle. I was afraid for the children and terrified for myself. I backed off, pulling the cradle and rocking it back and forth, but this just made the snakes pursue all the more fiercely. Then one of the children caught sight of the serpents, and lunging from the cradle he suddenly attacked them, grasping one in each hand.

Plautus *Amphitryon* 5.1

That a babe only a few days old could use large serpents as cradle toys (irreparably crushing them in the process) meant that his ancestry could hardly be disguised for long. Therefore, futile as it might be, the attempt had to be made to appease Hera, and both gods and men gave it a go.

Alcmene had named the infant Alcides - a combination word formed from Alaceus, the father of Amphitryon and Tiryns, the town where he was born. (That latter town remains today, its walls still standing, though considerably battered by the passage of thirty-one centuries.) Now Alcmene changed that name to 'Heracles'. This, the Greek form of 'Hercules', means 'glory of the Lady'. ('Hera' means 'Lady', being the feminine form of the word 'Hero'.) However, the bastard child of her husband's extra-marital affairs did not make the Goddess feel very glorified. In fact the name drew attention to her humiliation, and succeeded only in making Hera all the more furious.

Alcmene's ham-fisted attempt at flattery had backfired, but the attempt of the Gods did not do much better. By some accounts the plan was devised by Athena, which shows that even the Goddess of Wisdom can have her off days. The idea was that Hermes would smuggle the child into the heavens, and lay the babe at the side of the sleeping Hera. Hera would awaken to find that she was feeding a suckling child, and hopefully the experience would awaken her maternal instincts, making her more benevolent toward the child. And even if Hera's instincts failed to kick in, the child might at least get a mouthful of Hera's milk. This milk, combined with the child's divine ancestry, would further contribute towards making Hercules a demi-god.

Sure enough, when Hera awakened she was considerably confused at finding a foundling baby at her breast. From sympathy with the child's evident hunger she allowed him to keep feeding; that is, until the strength and vigour with which the baby extracted her milk caused Hera to figure out whose child was doing the extracting. With this realization, Hera wrenched the child away so violently that her milk jetted away across the skies. That milk remains in the heavens today. The Via Lactea, the Romans called it – 'the Milky Way'. In Greek this is 'the circle of milk', *galaxias kyklo*s – the galaxy.

Hera the unwitting wet-nurse
Sculpture by Johan Niclas Byströmin in the Royal Palace, Stockholm

Chapter 2

Growing pains

Alcmene was not unnaturally distressed at having incurred the enmity of a powerful goddess through no fault of her own. To make things worse Amphitryon had yet again managed to upset the hosts of the city in which he was staying. Exiled once more, the couple made their way to Thebes in central Greece.

To the left of the Elektran Gate are the remains of a house. They say here Amphitryon came to live when exiled from Tiryns ... and the rooms of Alcmene are still plainly to be seen among the ruins.
Pausanias *Guide to Greece* 9. 11. 1

Once settled in her new home, Alcmene decided that her only hope was to abandon the child who had so comprehensively ruined her life. The method she chose was exposure, a process brutally described by one historian as 'post-natal birth control'. In the ancient world there was no reliable form of birth control so unwanted children were common enough. The usual practice was to place these children in a field, a market, or by the city gates and let anyone who wanted adopt the child as though it were a stray kitten. If not picked up in time, the baby would perish from hunger and exposure to the elements.

How Zeus would have reacted to this maltreatment of his offspring is unknown, for Athena was the first to note this potentially disastrous development. Perhaps Athena felt a bit guilty that her plan to bring Hera around had been only partly successful. (Hera still loathed Hercules, but he had absorbed some of her milk, and was therefore officially a demi-god). Either for this reason, or because Athena always had something of a soft spot for rogues with a thuggish streak, the goddess was to become something of a mentor to Hercules now and in later years.

She retrieved the babe from the field where Alcmene had left him and restored him to his mother, possibly with a salutary warning not to repeat the attempt. About a thousand years later, a writer called Pausanias wrote the world's first travel guide for the benefit of ancient Roman tourists visiting Greece. Outside Thebes he directs the attention of the traveller to a field that was still called 'The field of Heracles' where this incident took place. (Pausanias 9.25.2). From here another poet takes up the tale of Hercules' boyhood.

The son of Amphitryon of Argos grew before his mother's eyes like a sapling plant set in a vineyard. He learned his letters from a sleepless mentor, a hero, the son of Apollo, the aged Linus. To bend a bow and shoot arrows at the mark, this he learned from Eurytus, a man born to wealth and great domains... and all the tricks and falls of the wrestlers of Argos, and of boxers adroit with the hand-strap, and all the cunning inventions and the give-and-take of fighters that roll upon the ground, all these he learned from a son of Hermes, Autolycus of Phanotè.
Theocritus *Idyll* 24.103

Interestingly it was Alcmene, rather than Amphitryon who selected these tutors, the best that the era could produce. Later ages were to see Hercules as a solitary hero who conducted solo missions. However, the ancient Greeks also knew Hercules as no mean general and commander, a man who led armies and conquered cities. These skills Hercules learned from a man called Castor, who may or may not have been the demigod who today makes up the 'Castor' part of the constellation of Gemini ('The Twins' - the other twin being Pollux). Castor taught Hercules 'How to marshal a company, measure an advancing squadron of the enemy and give orders to his own troop of horse.'

In other words, Hercules received the typical education of a young aristocratic male. Not the education of an aristocrat of his time, because in his day the universe was too rough and ready for things like formal educational curricula - Hercules' education was that of the later aristocrats who heard his legends declaimed in the theatre or to the music of a lyre. Aristocratic Graeco-Roman boys had to learn the arts of war, and also the arts of music and poetry.

They had also to learn the more pragmatic art of estate management, and perhaps this Hercules acquired from his step-father Amphitryon. Certainly it was from Amphitryon that Hercules learned that other essential skill of a Greek aristocrat - how to race a chariot. We also learn that Hercules and Amphitryon became close, and Hercules even moved his bed to share a room with his stepfather. Hercules was thus accepted as one of the leaders among the young men of his adoptive city.

The Hercules family at home
detail from a 1st century AD Roman painting found at Pompeii

As far as I know, the following is still the custom in Thebes [i.e. in AD 150 when this was written]. *A boy, who must be handsome, strong and of noble birth, is chosen priest of Isthmian Apollo for a year. He is called the Laurel-bearer, for the boys wear laurel wreaths* [the laurel was sacred to Apollo] . *I can't definitely claim that all the laurel bearers follow the custom of dedicating a bronze tripod to the God; in fact most probably don't, because when I was*

there I did not see that many votive tripods. But the wealthier boys certainly dedicate them. The most remarkable, both for its age and for the fame of the person who dedicated it, is a tripod given by Amphitryon on behalf of Heracles after he had worn the laurel.
Pausanias *Guide to Greece* 9.10.4

We note that all the teachers of Hercules were powerful and feared – when in their prime. Now they are aged, and in their declining years they act as tutors to the young Hero, who inherits their talents, mixing the different skills together to create within himself the sum of all their abilities. Regrettably, not all the skills were acquired in the same measure, for not even his most powerful advocates ever described Hercules as a scholar and a gentleman.

The only stringed instrument with which Hercules ever became truly proficient was the bow. This caused great frustration to Linus, the young man's music teacher. Linus was renowned as the inventor of melody, and had the misfortune to waste his genius on a student who could not carry a tune in a bucket. The final, particularly difficult, session ended with Linus giving his obtuse student a mighty wallop with his lyre. This blow the youth returned with interest. An unremarkable teacher-student contra-temps perhaps, except that Hercules did not hold back the mighty strength he had developed even then. Linus was squished like a grape.

Though gone, Linus has not been forgotten. He has given his name to a remarkable range of characters, from the second pope in Rome (the successor to St Peter) to a character in the Charlie Brown comic books. He is also the namesake of Linus Torvals, and as such can be found in the computer operating system which bears his name; Linux.

For removing such a memorable personage from the earth, Hercules was charged with homicide. Nor was Linus the first of the dozens of corpses whom Hercules was to leave strewn across the landscape of myth. There are suggestions that he also killed another of his tutors, though this was assumed to have been an accident. At his trial for killing Linus, the young Hercules testified in his own defence, maintaining that he had merely struck back at Linus to defend himself from further abuse.

This argument convinced the judges, but it carried less weight with Amphitryon. Hercules' step-father had worked out that the rapidly diminishing supply of tutors was due less to ill-fortune than to his stepson's ill-temper.

Accordingly Hercules was removed from his highly-cultured curriculum and rusticated to a cattle farm in the deep countryside where any damage he might do would be correspondingly limited. The ancient writer Apollodorus summarizes the incident thus:

Linus was the brother of Orpheus; he came to Thebes and became a Theban, but was slain through being struck with the lyre of Heracles. Because, after he had received a blow from Linus, Heracles flew into a rage and killed him. When tried for murder, Heracles quoted a law of Rhadamanthys, who laid it down that whoever defends himself against a wrongful aggressor shall go free. Thus he was acquitted. But fearing he might repeat the deed, Amphitryon sent him to a cattle farm.
Apollodorus *Library* 2.4.9

At this time the young man faced a choice. Apart from killing a tutor (or two) he had as yet done nothing with his life. Yet already he was aware that his unnatural strength was a gift from the Gods. Given how strength was venerated in heroic Greece, his physical prowess was as good as money in the bank. Added to that, he came from solidly aristocratic stock, even if one disregarded the reports of his divine parentage. He had missed out on the chance to become king of Mycenae, but there was nothing to prevent Hercules from becoming a wealthy cattle baron, extraordinary only through being considerably stronger than the bulls his herdsmen tended.

So should the young Hercules attempt to emulate, or even surpass the deeds of his great ancestor Perseus, and gain glory through danger and pain?

Or should he spend his life relaxing in pleasant indolence, and (to quote a later poet) with 'Vacant heart and hand and eye/Easy live and quiet die'? *(The Bride of Lammermoor,* by Walter Scott).

This dilemma took physical form for the young Hercules. The tale of what transpired is told by Xenophon, that same man who in 399 BC led the march of the Ten Thousand in one of the great adventures of Greek military history. In his memoirs, the old general relates the story of the 'Choice of Hercules':

He [Hercules] *took himself to a quiet place and there sat to contemplate. As he pondered which path to take, he saw two women approaching. Both were of*

unnaturally large stature, but one was fair and proud. Her limbs were pure, and her eyes were modest. Austere was her figure, and her robe was white.

The other was plump and soft from good meals. Make-up emphasised the natural white and pink of her face, and her clothing exaggerated her height and displayed rather than hid her charms. Doe-eyed, she admired herself and her own shadow, before quickly glancing about to see who else might have noticed her.

The first kept up her even pace as she approached, but the other pushed past, eager to be there first. 'Heracles, I see that you considering which path of life you should take. Befriend me. Follow me, and your road will be pleasant and easy. You will never know hardship, and all the sweet things of life will be yours. Forget wars and worries – your cares will be what choice food or drink you prefer, and what sights and sounds most delight you. What touch or perfume most pleases, whose tender love you most enjoy, what bed yields the softest slumbers; and how little effort you need expend to obtain these.'

'You'll never need worry you can't afford your luxuries, or fear that I'll make you win them by straining body and soul in effort. Others will do the work for you, and hold back nothing. Those who follow me have my permission to take whatever they want.'

On hearing this Heracles asked 'Please tell me, Lady, what is your name?'

She replied 'My friends call me Happiness. Those who hate me call me Vice.'

All the while the other had kept up her approach. Now she too spoke. 'I also have come for you, Hercules. I know your parents and have followed your education. It is my hope that you will take the road that leads to me. You will become one who does great and noble things, and in doing them through my gifts, I too will become more illustrious and honoured. But let not this pleasant introduction deceive you – I intend to talk plainly about the way things are, and how the Gods have decreed they must be. '

'For the Gods have decreed that nothing worthwhile comes to man but that he works to earn it. To earn the favour of the Gods, you must worship the Gods. Desiring the love of friends, you must do good for them … and if you want your body to be strong, you must make it the servant of your mind, and train it with effort and sweat.'

Hearing this, Vice remarked, 'You hear what this woman says, Heracles?

The road to joy is hard and long. Let me take you down the short and easy path to happiness.'

And Virtue retorted, 'You poor creature. What good thing is yours, or what worthwhile knowledge, if you have done nothing to earn it? You can't even wait for desire, but get things before you want them. You eat before you are hungry and drink before you are thirsty. ... You are wanton by night, and waste in sleep the best of the day. Immortal, you are the outcast of the Gods and the scorn of good men.

'Praise is sweetest of all things to hear, but hear it you never will. Nor will you ever see that sweetest of all sights – a good job done by yourself. ... What sane man dares join your ranks? While young, your followers are weak. When old, their souls have no foundation. Idle and sleek, they thrive in youth, becoming withered and weary as they journey to old age. Past deeds bring shame, present deeds, distress. They burned through pleasure while young, but saved up hardship for their old age.'

'My company is with Gods and good men, and they do nothing worthwhile without me. ... Craftsmen call me a beloved workmate, I faithfully guard the home and protect the servants within; a helper in peace, an ally in war, the best partner of friendship. ...'

'Come the appointed end, my followers lie not forgotten and dishonoured. They live for all time in memory and song. Heracles, son of noble parents, work for me in this way, and genuine happiness will be yours.'
Xenophon *Memorabilia* 2.1.21-34

Xenophon assumes all of posterity knows which Lady Hercules chose to follow. If contemporaries were uncertain, two incidents in Hercules' eighteenth year made his position clear. Amphitryon had settled in lands farthest east of that part of Greece dominated by Thebes, an area adjacent to the little kingdom of Thespis and hard against the Cythairon mountain range which later formed the natural border between Athens and Thebes - or between Attica and Boeotia to give these territories their proper names.

The mountains were steep and sinister ('no corner of Cythairon is echoless' claims Sophocles in his play *Oedipus Rex*). From these resounding and shadowy gorges came a great lion, a monster that feasted upon the herds of Amphitryon and the flocks of the people of Thespis. Many humans also fell victim to this relentless predator. Some were herdsmen who were devoured along with their cattle, and others were nobles who set out to hunt the mighty beast and ended by feeding it. So perished Euippus, prince of Thebes, and his death inspired the young Hercules. Hercules was, after all, in charge of the cattle right in the lion's main feeding grounds. For the newest follower of Virtue, the path of duty led straight to the lion's den.

The Cythairon mountain range was no easy place to hunt. It is more than ten miles from end to end, and offers an endless variety of places for even a large lion to hide itself. For his expedition, Hercules needed a base closer to the mountains than his home ranch. This he obtained by taking up residence with the king of Thespis. At this time the king of Thespis was better known than the young Hercules, though as a lover, not a fighter. Through prodigious over-achievement in his given area of endeavour, the Thespian king had produced not one, not ten, but fifty daughters of nubile age. Perhaps so substantial a contribution to the population of heroic Greece had given the king an interest in eugenics, for he came up with a cunning plan.

While the (alleged) son of Amphitryon was currently unknown for anything apart from his ambition to take down a murderous lion, the young Hercules was already an impressive sight. He stood four cubits-and-a-foot tall in his sandals, and was so muscular that at first glance he appeared small of stature. (By comparison Goliath was six cubits tall when slain by David some five generations later. A cubit is 45 cm or a foot-and-a-half.) He was, incidentally, a blond. This we discover from a brief reference in Euripides to the lion-skin helmet of Hercules 'hiding his yellow hair'. (Euripides *The Madness of Heracles* 1.359)

Therefore, when the king of Thespis suggested to Hercules that his elder daughter might keep the hero company at night after each long day of hunting, both Hercules and daughter endorsed the idea.

Eventually Hercules got the lion, though the story of the actual take-down is lost. The event might have been a ferocious hand-to-fang encounter, though this need not necessarily have been so. As well as being skilled at fighting at close quarters, Hercules was a dab hand with a javelin and unequalled as an archer. But most probably that the deed was done with the blunt instrument which became Hercules' trademark.

Our hero's hunt took him to Mt Helicon, the most distinguished of all the peaks in the Cythairon range. Helicon was sacred to the Muses, and there Hercules might have drunk the waters of the Hippocrene spring, which welled from the flanks of the mountain where it had been struck by the hooves of the winged horse Pegasus. On that mountain, Hercules found a tough, gnarled olive tree with wood of singular hardness. He uprooted the tree, and fashioned it into a club.

It was this club which in later years became Hercules' standard manner of introducing himself to the monsters and villains of his era. So proud were the Thebans of their adoptive son that a thousand years later it was the image of this same club that adorned hoplite shields when the Thebans went to war. However, while it may be presumed that the Cythairon lion was the club's first victim, the story of that climatic part of the lion hunt has been lost; overshadowed by a later revelation - that the king of Thespis had not been completely honest with Hercules.

Thespius was king of Thespis, and Hercules stayed with him when he went to kill the lion. The king was his host for fifty days. Every night, after Hercules returned from the hunt, Thespius sent one of his daughters to sleep with him. He was eager that his daughters should have children by Hercules. And Hercules thought that he was sleeping with the same girl, but actually had sex with all of them.
Apollodorus *Library* 2.4.10

This deception is somewhat more credible when we recall that among the Graeco-Roman peoples who heard the legend, nice girls did it with the lights off. In fact the poet Martial, writing in the Roman imperial era, complained of a girlfriend who was up for anything, anywhere, so long as her boyfriend couldn't see it happening. So between days spent trekking through the mountains and dark evenings of passion, Hercules may have been startled by the initiative and enduring enthusiasm of his paramour, but he lacked the energy to explore the matter further.

This statue of the young Hercules suggests that the daughters of Thespius might not have been completely opposed to their father's scheme
Roman statue of Hercules currently in the Metropolitan Museum of Art, New York

23

In fact the king was successful beyond his wildest dreams, for so mightily did Hercules rise to the challenge that he left behind fifty pregnant ex-girlfriends. These children became founder members of a tribe known as the Heracleidae, those (very numerous) descendants of Hercules who were later to sweep across the Peloponnese and forever end the struggle between Pelopids and Perseids in the latter's favour.

The impregnation of fifty girls in fifty nights while engaged in an arduous hunt for a monster lion during the days was referred to by later Greeks as the 'thirteenth Labour of Hercules'. Technically of course, it was the 0th labour, but while the Greeks had no shortage of nit-picking pedants, they lacked the concept of zero as a number. Therefore they had to tack this initial feat to the end of the sequence. To the Greeks of his day, his feats in Cythairon had made Hercules a man to watch - especially by the fathers of teenage daughters.

Our hero had hit his stride, and he showed no signs of slowing down. His second adventure met Hercules even before he had returned home and washed the dust of the mountains out of his newly-grown beard. Just before the gates of Thebes, he came across ambassadors from Orchomenus.

Orchomenus was at that time the most powerful city in the region, home to the Minyans. The Minyans were an ancient people who pre-dated the more recent stock among whom Alcmene and the Thebans were numbered. Archaeologists have suggested that the connection between the Minyans and the Minoans may be as close as the name suggests. The Minoan culture dominated the sea-faring states of the bronze-age Aegean, and while Orchomenus was not actually a Minoan colony, it may have had very close links with that powerful civilization.

Certainly the Minyans were not a people to offend, yet that was exactly what the Thebans had done. A Theban chariot, driven at speed beside the temple of Poseidon, had thrown up a stone which struck and killed the Minyan king. In recompense, Orchomenus demanded tribute of a hecatomb of cattle every year for twenty years. (A hecatomb was the standard unit of cattle, being 120 of the beasts.)

Being a rancher himself, and well aware of the difficulties involved in raising cattle in those dangerous times, Hercules inquired mildly whether a hecatomb was not a trifle excessive for a minor city such as Thebes was at that time. Arrogantly, the ambassadors replied that the hecatomb was an example of their city's amazing restraint. Properly speaking, they should have taken not just the cattle, but the noses and ears of the Thebans as well.

This was the wrong answer to give a proud and powerful young man who considered himself Theban by adoption. The ambassadors set off home to Orchomenus with their noses and ears removed and strung around their necks. To ensure these horrible garlands were not removed, Hercules took the ambassadors' hands off as well. He then informed his victims that this was all the tribute that they would carry from Thebes that year.

Three sanctuaries stand along the road from the Neistan gate. That of Heracles is furthest off, in an open space. Here Hercules is called 'the nose trimmer', the Thebans explaining that the reason for the name is that Heracles cut off the noses of the heralds who came from Orkhomenos to demand the tribute.
Pausanias, *Guide to Greece* 9. 25. 4

The reaction from Orchomenus was predictably swift and indignant. A squadron of chariots swept down upon the city demanding the immediate surrender of the impudent youth who had mutilated their ambassadors. Creon, the Theban king, felt he had little choice but to obey. When their king had been accidentally killed, the Minyans had marched on his city and killed not a few Thebans before they were brought off with the promise of tribute. As well as cattle, the Minyans had taken the armour and weapons of the Thebans in order to keep them suitably subservient. Creon must have reasoned that if his city had not been able to withstand the Minyans before, when they were properly armed, what chance did his people have now that they were almost defenceless? Accordingly he sent men to seek Hercules and hand him over to his city's oppressors. By now night had fallen, and the young hero was no-where to be found. He was out of town, further building his legend.

Chapter 3

Triumph and madness

More precisely, Hercules was out sabotaging the Orchomenan chariot horses, and in the process gaining another name that would stick with him through antiquity; Hippodetus, 'the horse stringer'. Early Greece, and indeed, the entire ancient world had absolutely no concept of animal rights. So when Hercules sneaked by night into the corral where the enemy horses were being kept, and made the chariots useless by hamstringing the unfortunate horses which pulled them, this was seen as a cunning ploy with no unhappy side-effects. Without their dreaded chariots, the Minyans were simply a small group of infantry with inadequate and unsuitable weapons.

But the Minyans at least had weapons, which is more than could be said for the Thebans. However, Hercules had thought of that too. As word of his latest exploit swept the city, the young men repudiated the peace made by King Creon and demanded to be led against their oppressors.

'Go to the temples', Hercules told them, 'and there seize the weapons and armour dedicated by past generations of Theban warriors.'

This may have caused a degree of uncertainty among even the most hot-headed and war-like of the young men. These weapons were sacred to the Gods, for it was the custom of warriors who had done great things in war to surrender their arms to their patron god or goddess in return for the favour of the God had shown to them in battle. So the weapons in the temples were the property of the Olympian Gods.

Given that war with Orchomenus was going to be a chancy business at best, would it really be a good idea to start by alienating the very Gods on whose favour the city depended for survival?

If ever Hercules needed the support of his divine father, it was now, at this early point of his career. Without a sign that the Gods favoured Thebes and were happy for their armour to be used in the city's cause, Hercules would have been little more than a footnote in the long epic of the Heroic Age - a rash young man who brought about the destruction of Thebes by wildly over-estimating his own abilities. Fortunately, for once father Zeus was on hand to protect his son. That the Gods consented to the Thebans arming themselves was demonstrated by the fact that the Gods themselves armoured Hercules, providing the hero with the most splendid panoply of armour and weapons yet seen in the young world.

So magnificent was the armour, and so evidently was it of divine origin that the would-be warriors of Thebes abandoned their reservations and flocked to the temples to arm themselves with whatever was available.

At this point, the writer must yield the page to the poet Hesiod, who in the eighth century BC, wrote of these events. Hercules is about to don his divine armour and lead his rag-tag army into battle. Like any self-respecting warrior of his day, and just as the Greeks of two generations later were to do before the walls of Troy, Hercules was going to war on a chariot. He begins by addressing his chariot driver;

'Iolaus, rough battle is now close at hand. Do now as you have done so skilfully before, help me as you can and turn Arion, our great black-maned horse, speedily in every direction.'
Hesiod *The Shield of Heracles* l.115ff

The name of this chariot driver is perplexing, for Iolaus was the son of Hercules' half-brother Iphicles. Like Hercules, Iphicles was not yet out of his teenage years, and even at his most precocious, Iphicles could not have fathered a son more than six years old. It would be somewhat premature to put such a child at the controls of an instrument of war that for the ancient world was something between a battle tank and a high-powered sports car - especially as one of the horses was Arion.

Arion is the first-mentioned of Hercules' set of divine weaponry, for he was no ordinary horse - and controlling him was no task for an amateur. Black-maned Arion was the child of two Gods — Poseidon and Demeter. The legend says that earth-shaking Poseidon, the Lord of the Sea, was gripped by an incestuous lust for his sister Demeter, Goddess of the Corn. Demeter tried to escape her brother's attentions by taking the form of a mare hiding in a herd of horses. This was an unwise choice, for Poseidon is also God of Horses, and swiftly located the beast that was not one of his own. Swiftly changing his form to a stallion, he found Demeter and mounted her as a hapless mare before she could escape. From this forced union was born Arion.

Bronze age chariot and driver
Detail from a contemporary vase in the Metropolitan Museum of Art, New York

(Some academics will suggest that such a myth might arise, for example, from an earthquake-induced tsunami [Poseidon] flooding a cornfield [Demeter]. Having been salted by seawater, the land was then used to produce horses [Arion]. But we should scorn such mundane explanations and simply celebrate Arion, his huge size and prodigious strength.)

In vain do the east and west winds race against him. No less swiftly does he carry the son of Amphitryon in his wars ... fierce even with him also and impatient of control.'

So says the Roman poet Statius (*Thebaid* 6). Indeed Arion was definitely no My Little Pony for a six-year-old Iolaus. Therefore it may be best to assume that Iolaus, son of Iphicles, was named in honour of this charioteer who served Hercules so nobly that day.

Heracles, he put greaves of shining bronze upon his legs. These were the splendid gift of Hephaestus.
Hesiod l.122 *ibid*

Greaves were a sort of footless rigid metal sock worn between ankle and knee. The huge Greek battle shield protected everything from knee to throat, but - as Achilles was later to discover - protection for the lower extremities was also a good idea. Some warriors wore just the one greave, on the leg pushed forward in the battle-line, but Hercules could afford a full pair. His were made by Hephaestus, the Craftsman God of Olympus and maker of the finest armour on heaven and earth. It is just as well that Hephaestus and his mother were not on speaking terms at that point. For Hephaestus was the son of Hera, and having her *bête-noir* armoured by her own offspring probably did little to improve child-parent relations.

Next he [Hercules] *fastened a cunningly-made golden breastplate, the gift Pallas Athena, the daughter of Zeus. ... Over his shoulders the mighty warrior put that armour that saves men from death, and he slung his hollow quiver over his back. Within were many death-dealing arrows ... the shafts smooth and very long; and at the end fletched with the feathers of a brown eagle. And he took his strong spear, with its point of shining bronze. And on his heroic head he sat a well-made helm, diamond-hard, which closely fitted his temples and guarded that god-like brow.*
l.125ff *ibid*

According to the writer Apollodorus (second century BC) the bow was a gift from Apollo, and though not mentioned here, Hercules also sported a sword given by Hermes to complement the olive-tree club and marvellous shield which rounded off his personal arsenal.

In his hands he took his glittering shield, which none ever broke or crushed with a blow. It was a wonder to see, shimmering with enamel, white ivory and electrum, and glowing with shining gold ... deadly Fate was pictured there holding one man newly wounded, and another unwounded. One, who was dead, she was dragging by the feet through the tumult. She wore on her shoulders a garment red with human blood, and terrifyingly she glared and gnashed her teeth.
l.139ff *ibid*

There is a whole genre in classical poetry which describes the shields of the great heroes of legend. Achilles had one, and Aeneas another - not just shields, but huge works of art laden with symbolism. Indeed, to contain all the subjects described, each shield must have been large enough to roof a substantial building. Among the sporting scenes, battle scenes, festival scenes, besieged cities, harbours, pastoral scenes and parades of gods and heroes which Hercules' shield portrayed in great detail was a depiction of Hercules' ancestor, Perseus

There, too, was the horseman Perseus, son of rich-haired Danae ... with winged sandals on his feet, and his black-sheathed sword hanging from his shoulders on a cross-belt of bronze. Swift as thought he flew, the head of the monster, the dreaded Gorgon on his broad back in a bag of silver wondrous to see, from which hung bright tassels of gold. On the hero's head was the dreadful cap of Hades; dark as the gloomiest night.
l.216ff *ibid*

The shield showed the world of Hercules, with its people at work, at war and at play. And with the shield, so was the world of Hercules;

Around the rim flowed Ocean in full stream, enclosing all the cunning work of the shield. Here swans soared and called loudly, and others were numerous, swimming upon the water; with shoals of fish nearby. The great, strong shield

was a wonder to behold – even for loud-thundering Zeus at whose orders Hephaestus had made and fitted it. The valiant son of Zeus expertly bore this shield as, agile and fast as the lightning of his father, he leapt upon his chariot. L.314ff *ibid*

After the wordy descriptions of Hercules in all his martial finery, the actual campaign against the Minyans is usually dismissed in a few brief sentences, as though the main achievement of Hercules in this short war was to get dressed for it.

According to myth, Thebes was beside an ancient lake - in fact the hero Cadmus founded the city after killing the water dragon which guarded it. This bemused Greeks of the classical era who knew of no such lake, but modern geology has proven the myth-mongers correct, and shown that beside pre-archaic Thebes there was indeed originally a lake which was later drained.

When the king of the Minyans descended on Thebes with his army, he was met by Hercules and his Theban minute-men 'at a narrow place'. (Diodorus Siculus 4.10.5) This was probably between this lake and the mountains. The narrowness of the battlefield served the Thebans as the equally constrained field of Thermopylae served the 300 Spartans in later centuries. Huge as the enemy host might be, its soldiers were forced to line up to enter the battle in an orderly fashion, for there was no room for them to all be deployed at once. On reaching the front of the line, the Minyan warriors met Hercules in his wrath and were promptly mown down.

The battle was more equal in those parts of the field not dominated by Hercules. Most accounts agree that it was here, while holding the Theban battle-line in place, that Amphitryon the step-father of Hercules, was slain while fighting heroically. The writers of later tragic plays have been unable to bear the loss of so powerful a character from the stage of Hercules' later life. Therefore they insist that he survived, so after this battle we must consider Amphitryon as being rather like Schroedinger's cat; simultaneously alive or dead depending on the circumstances.

If Amphitryon fell in the battle, then poetic justice demanded that someone of equal worth must die on the other side. Poetic justice is very powerful in a story told by poets, so in those versions in which Amphitryon bites the dust ('bites the dust' being a quote from Homer's *Iliad*, Book 2, line 369), the king of the Minyans must die also. In those versions where

Amphitryon survives, so does the king of the Minyans, though as a captive of the victorious Thebans. The Minyan king made a peace with Hercules by which the tribute that had caused the war was now doubled, but was payable by the Minyans to Thebes, rather than the other way around.

In the grimmer version of the tale, the Minyan king and his army were slaughtered, and Hercules and his men helped themselves to the weapons, armour and battle standards of the slain. As dusk fell they arrived at Orchomenus looking like the victorious army that they actually were. The Minyans naturally but mistakenly assumed that this was their army, returned from crushing the impertinent Thebans. Trustingly, they let the soldiers into the city. In this version of the story, the Minyans paid no tribute to the Thebans at the end of the war, because once Hercules and his men were done with their city, there was no Orchomenus and no Minyans left to pay anything.

Thus, even as word of slaying of the lion of Cythairon spread through Greece, hard on the heels of that report came another telling of Hercules' feats as a great general, armed and armoured by the Gods, the young hero who had humbled mighty Orchomenus.

Suddenly Hercules had stepped into the ranks of the leading warriors of his day, and had become a man whom even the king of Thebes would be proud to call a son. So a prince of Thebes Hercules duly became, because the king gave to Hercules the hand of his eldest daughter, Megara, in marriage.

(There is some dispute as to how Megara came to have the name of a Greek city north-east of Athens. Was the city named after the legendary character, or was the bride was named after the city, for Megara has been settled since very ancient times?)

However the bride got her name, none dispute that the marriage of Hercules to Megara was happy. Our hero temporarily abandoned his career of slaughter to settle down as a husband and father. The couple took up residence in the home of the widowed/still happily married Alcmene and settled down to produce an expanding brood of children.

How long this period of domestic bliss endured is uncertain, and can only be roughly estimated by the varying accounts of the number of children born into the family. Since there were three to eight children, depending which poet was doing the counting, we can guess that this interlude of serenity lasted somewhere between five years and a decade.

Even as the count of the children in the Hercules family varies, so do accounts of what happened next. Once again we are forced to go with the general consensus while noting outliers from the standard tale, such as the radically different version of the playwright Euripides – but then scriptwriters have ever put the demands of a paying audience ahead of adherence to the actual narrative.

Everyone agrees that the spell of herculean happiness was brought to an end by the malice of Hera. She had not forgotten her feud with the son born of her husband's adulterous affair, and that man's continued well-being was a daily reproach to her ability to conduct a decent vendetta. However, Zeus was currently well-pleased with Hercules, so in order to get back to ruining Hercules' life, Hera had first to subvert the hero's mighty protector.

Hercules, Megara and child
Adapted from the 4th century Asteas Vase (Museo Arqueologico Nacional, Madrid)

Hera did this by pointing out that in those early years after the beginning of the world, the place was, frankly, a mess. Unlike more structured versions of the creation, the world of Greek myth had not sprung into being through the methodical efforts of a *faber deus* (as those who study myth refer to a 'Creator God'). Rather the mythical world had emerged willy-nilly into being, with matter coalescing into shape from chaos. This emergence had been completely random, and some of the creatures which had emerged were hugely powerful, violently destructive and downright anti-social.

Those monsters capable of actually destroying the cosmos Zeus and his cohorts had stopped - though not without effort. This nevertheless left a host of creatures running around the world of mythology, wreaking havoc despite the best efforts of the current generation of heroes - a band ever shrinking in number due to the contingencies of the job. (Even the supposedly unkillable Cauneus was to die in battle, nailed upright into the ground by a demented centaur who used a tree-trunk as a hammer.)

Zeus had not created the Earth, nor was he responsible for it. He and his brothers had divided the cosmos between them, with Poseidon taking the sea, Hades the Underworld, and Zeus the heavens. No-one ruled the Earth, not least because the Earth was a mighty goddess in herself - Gaia, the grandmother of Zeus and of most other Olympian gods.

However, as Hera pointed out, monsters rampaging around grandma's place made Zeus look bad, and upset the many mortals who looked to Zeus for protection. Fundamentally, Zeus was the God of Order, which is why he had the government of Gods and men in his charge. Yet the Earth was looking pretty disorganized. Not only was Zeus doing nothing about this, but there was his allegedly mighty son, of whose potential Zeus had so often boasted. What had the man contributed lately - he whose mightiest labour these days was to change the diapers on his infant babes?

The King of the Gods acknowledged that his wife had a point, and prepared to summon Hercules back to his heroic duties. However, persuading Zeus to put Hercules back to work was only the first part of Hera's diabolical scheme. By an unlikely coincidence, at that very moment Hercules received a summons from his cousin, Eurystheus, King of Mycenae. As the dominant power in the region Mycenae could call on heroes such as Hercules if the situation required it. Somehow, just at the moment Hera had been at work on Zeus, Eurystheus had decided that there was heroing to be done, and that Hercules should do it.

Eurystheus viewed the growing power of Heracles with suspicion, and summoned him to his court intending there to order him to perform certain tasks. Hercules ignored the command until Zeus sent a message ordering him

to serve the will of Eurystheus. At this Heracles journeyed to Delphi, to confirm the matter by asking the Gods directly. The oracle replied that it was the will of the Gods that Heracles should perform twelve Labours under the supervision of Eurystheus. Should he complete these, he would be rewarded with immortality. This development deeply depressed Heracles. He thought of his great achievements to date, and felt that because of these he did not deserve to have his work overseen by one he considered beneath him. Yet he also saw that he would harm himself if he did not obey Zeus, who was also his father.
Diodorus Siculus 4.10 -11.

Hercules was a proud man - indeed, this was one of his defining characteristics. Whether or not he suspected that Eurystheus had pre-empted him in taking the Mycenaean throne through an unfairly premature birth, Hercules doubtless considered Eurystheus a Pelopid. Given his own noble ancestry through Pursues, Hercules felt it demeaning to enter into the service of a family whose domination of the Peloponnese his Perseid clan had spent generations resisting. So he dithered, and his delay in obeying the clearly-stated orders of the Gods gave Hera the chance to strike a wicked blow.

Though his chronology is suspect, the playwright Euripides gives the best account of what happened next. Even as Hera schemed on Mount Olympus, matters political had been developing in Hercules' home town of Thebes. While Hercules was away at Delphi, the king of Thebes was overthrown by a usurper. This usurper was Lycus, a son of the Sea God, Poseidon. Lycus noted that princess Megara, wife of Hercues, had children of her own. Being of the former king's direct line these children had a legitimate claim to his throne. Therefore, as a matter of dynastic principle, Lycus' power would not be secure until the children and their mother were executed. (And Amphitryon as well, this being one of those occasions when he was not dead.)

To ensure that the killing went went smoothly, the usurper king decided to oversee the executions in person. As things turned out, this proved to be unwise. Hercules returned home from Delphi just as the execution squad was preparing to go about its grim business. The hero was surprised and indignant to see his family dressed in funeral robes. He demanded to be brought up to speed on developments, and being Hercules, his demands were very hard to refuse. The news update was promptly followed by the shortest counter-revolution in Theban history.

Once the dust had settled, Megara's father was restored to the throne by a rejoicing populace and an unceremonious burial was given to such remains of Lycus as could be scraped from Hercules' front doorstep. All appeared to be well, so, in celebratory mode, the family settled down to a formal dinner to commemorate their narrow escape. Unbeknown to them, an invisible, uninvited guest was present at the occasion. This was Lyssa, the deity who brings madness. Reluctantly she followed Hera's orders, proclaiming:

I am the daughter of Night, born of noble parents from the blood of Uranus. The power I have, I use not in anger against friends, and nor do I take any pleasure in visiting the homes of men. ... . This man against whose house I am sent is famed in heaven and earth alike. I urge you; do not wish him awful harm ...

I call the sun-god to witness that what I do, I do against my will. But if indeed I must serve Hera and follow as hounds in full cry follow the huntsman, then follow I shall. And not the ocean with its moaning waves, nor the earthquake, nor the thunderbolt with its blast of pain will be half so furious as my headlong charge into the heart of Heracles.

Euripides *The Madness of Heracles* 1.842ff

A messenger survived to later carry the news to the city council chamber of Thebes, where he related the story to the stunned assembly:

'Sacrificial victims were in position before the altar of Zeus. The house needed to be purified, for there Heracles had cast from his hall and slain the [usurper] *king. His lovely children stood in a group, with his father* [Amphitryon] *and Megara; and already the basket was being passed round the altar, and we were keeping holy silence. But just as Alcmene's son had taken the torch in his right hand to dip in the holy water, he stopped without a word. His children looked up to see why their father delayed. And oh! He looked different. His bloodshot eyes rolled and bulged in their sockets; and foam dribbled down his bearded cheek.'*

'Eventually he spoke, all the while with a sort of demented chuckle. 'Father,

why should I sacrifice before I have slain Eurystheus? Why kindle the purifying flame only to have to do it again when I can end it all at a blow? As soon as I have brought here the head of Eurystheus, purification shall be done for all whom I have killed. Spill that water, toss away the baskets. Ha! Now give me my bow and club! I'm off to famous Mycenae. I'll need crow-bars and pick-axes, and with those iron levers I'll heave from their very foundations those city-walls ...'.

'And off he went. Though he had no chariot there, he thought he had, and mounted himself on a chair, using a whip on the 'horses' as though his fingers really held one. The bemused servants looked at each other asking, 'Is our master fooling around, or has he gone mad?'

...

'Eventually, while he uttered fearful threats against Eurystheus, his imagination brought him to Mycenae. Catching him by a muscular arm, his father demanded 'My son, what do you think you are doing? What does this bizarre conduct mean? Has the blood of your recent kills made you hysterical?'

But Heracles imagined it was the father of Eurystheus abjectly pleading to touch his hand. He shoved him aside, and thinking he was about to slay the sons of Eurystheus he prepared his quiver and aimed his bow at his own children. In wild panic they darted here and there. One buried himself in his hapless mother's skirts, another fled to the shadow of a pillar, while a third, like a bird, sought shelter beneath the altar.

The mother cried out, 'What are you doing? As a father do you mean to slay your children?' With his aged stepfather and servants crying aloud, Heracles hunted his child round and round the pillar in dreadful circles. Finally confronting the child, he shot him through the heart. The boy fell back, his last gasps of life spraying the stone column with blood. Then did Heracles shout for joy, boasting, 'That's one of Eurystheus' brood dead at my feet as atonement for his father's hate'.

'Then he turned his bow on the child who crouched at the altar's foot hoping to escape unseen. But before Heracles could loose his arrow, the poor child threw himself at his father's knees, flinging his hand upward to reach his beard or neck. 'Oh, I'm your child, your own. I'm no son of Eurystheus. Don't kill me, father!'

'Heracles frowned like a Gorgon, but his son stood too close for his baleful *archery. So he brought down his club and struck the boy on the head, even as a blacksmith hammers the red-hot iron. The second son caught, his bones smashed, he hurries to add a third victim to the pair. But before he could do so, the poor mother had grabbed her child, rushed into the house and shut the doors. Then the madman, as though he really were at the Cyclopean walls* [of Mycenae], *crowbars open the doors and throws the door-posts aside. Then with one evil bow-shot, he kills both wife and child.'*

'Rampaging on, he turns to slay his aged stepfather – but look! A phantom appeared (or so it seemed to we who looked on). It was Pallas Athena in her plumed helmet, brandishing a spear. She hurled a rock at Heracles which hit him on the chest and immediately quenched his frantic thirst for blood. Unconscious, he plunged to the ground, smacking his back into a column which had spilt in two and fallen to the floor when the roof caved in.'

'At that we stopped out panicked flight, and with the old man helping we tied him [Hercules] *tightly to the pillar so that when he came round he could do no further harm. And there he sleeps, the poor wretch, in a sleep that is anything but blessed. He's murdered his wife and children; and for myself I know of no son of man more miserable than he.'*

Euripides *The Madness of Heracles* l.922ff

Chapter 4

Hercules in labour

The world of archaic Greece took personal responsibility to much greater lengths than does the more forgiving modern era. Any modern court would take one look at the charge sheet and immediately exonerate Hercules of infanticide and murder. Not only do we have the confessions of the true perpetrators (Lyssa and Hera), but even at the time, impartial eyewitnesses immediately realized that Hercules was in the grip of insanity when he perpetrated the hideous deed. However, while he was patently innocent from a modern viewpoint, none of these excuses let our hero off the hook by the standards of his own day.

Those standards were simple. Hercules did it, so Hercules was guilty. Blameless - but guilty. In exactly the same way a generation later, Oedipus would blind himself in acknowledgement that he had killed his father and slept with his mother - this despite the fact that he had striven mightily to prevent those very deeds. One can see the point - in an age without proper forensic tools, it was all too easy for the perpetrator of a criminal act to pass responsibility to the influence of a malign god.

Furthermore, homicidal tendencies were only acceptable on the battlefield or in the course of everyday heroic activity. A slayer who was evidently and irredeemably deranged might be innocent, but must nevertheless be put down for the general safety of the community. The key term here is 'irredeemably deranged'. Hercules' future would be decided by his reaction when he regained consciousness, including whether he had a future at all.

Euripides takes up the tale once more with Amphitryon well aware of the risk that Hercules might remain homicidally insane when he came to. Amphitryon also knew that if this was the case, then Hercules would take some putting down. He cautions mourners;

Gently with your dirge of woe, old friends. Otherwise he might wake, break his chains and destroy the house, tear me to pieces, and then do the same to the city. ... Run, run, my aged friends! Escape his waking fury! For soon, as he runs amok through the streets of Thebes, he will pile fresh corpses upon those already slain.

Euripides *The Madness of Heracles* l.1055ff

To the relief of his audience, Hercules awakened from his sleep in full possession of his senses. There came now the painful task of updating him on what had happened during his madness. A child of his era, Hercules immediately acknowledged his own guilt.

Alas! Why do I spare my own life when I have taken that of my dear children? Perhaps I should rush to leap from a cliff, or maybe avenge having spilt my children's blood by driving a sword through my own heart. If I throw my body into the fire I shall at least avoid the infamy which would otherwise follow through my life.

...

Now my dearest friends will see me exposed to the pollution incurred by my children's murder. Ah, what am I to do? Where shall I find release from my misery? Shall I take wings [off a cliff] or plunge beneath the earth? I am so ashamed of the evil I have done. Now you must allow me to veil my head in the darkness of death. Fresh with new blood-guilt, I do not want to harm other innocents.

....

Why then should I go on living? What is the good of a useless, damned life? No! Let gorgeous Hera dance in bliss! Let Zeus' wife strike the sparkling floors of Olympus with her divine slipper! She has achieved her goal! She has toppled me in my prime, right down to the foundations. What man would pray to such a goddess? Her jealousy over her husband's visit to the bed of a mortal woman has driven her to destroy a blameless man who has done nothing but good for humanity.

Euripides *The Madness of Heracles* (l.1055- 1200 *passim*)

There are different accounts of what happened next. Since he was manifestly recovered from his insanity, the Thebans did not have the painful task of killing their hero in self-defence.

Nevertheless, Hercules was shunned for his guilt. According to some stories, Hercules remained at home, nursed through his depression by his parents. However, other texts agree that at this point Hercules embraced the sentiment that 'The gallant man endures without flinching the blows of heaven'. Aware of his blood-guilt, he exiled himself from Thebes and his home of ill-memory, and sought expiation in Athens. However, so great was his crime that only great deeds could clean the pollution from his soul. Again Delphi prompted Hercules to go to Mycenae, and there place himself in the service of Eurystheus.

According to some sources, it was only now that our hero gained the name 'Heracles'. By this version of the story, the Delphic oracle informed him that great glory would be earned through expunging the malice of Hera. This would be 'the glory of Hera' - that because of her vindictiveness, Hera's victim would become immortal in legend and earn a place in the heavens. Rather than destroying Hercules as intended, his name would make clear that Hera herself had made Hercules the legendary hero he would become.

This idea appealed to Hercules, and would have resonated with an audience familiar with the saying that to be avenged on his enemies, all a man need do was to prosper mightily.

It was hard to fight with a goddess, but the oracle had shown Hercules the way. He would become famous, nay, glorious, and by his name the world would know that it was Hera who had driven him to such epic success.

The evil deed Hera had inspired could not be undone, but it could be made to backfire on its perpetrator. Humbled, Hercules the child-killer would place himself in the power of Eurystheus, even as the Gods had ordained. Then, by the deeds he would perform Hercules would expiate his crime in such a fashion that the world would remember his name even after the name of Hera herself was half-forgotten.

The Labours of Hercules were an act of revenge.

Eurystheus

Father Zeus, Lord of the Lightning, I have hurried with news for your ear. This day a fine child has been born. He is called Eurystheus ('Broad

strength'), *son to Sthenelus son of Perseus; he is of your line; which is proper as he shall reign over the Greeks.'*
Hera to Zeus; Homer *Iliad* 19.122.

Eurystheus, king of Mycenae
Sketch from a 5th century red-figure vase now in the Louvre, Paris.

The king of Mycenae was not a happy man. The head that wears the crown is proverbially uneasy, and in this case it was doubly so, because the wearer of the crown was well aware that it should have been Hercules underneath the thing. Eurystheus had no easy job in any case, being a Pelopid in a land still sympathetic to the Perseids. The rise to fame of Hercules had caused disquiet to Eurystheus, and even greater disquiet was caused by the manner of that rise. If Hercules could lead the disarmed and defenceless Thebans to a crushing victory over the power of Orchomenus, what might he do later, when properly set up and ready to take 'his' throne by force from Eurystheus?

The fact that Hercules hated and despised him had raised a matching antipathy in Eurystheus. After all, Hercules was being more than somewhat hypocritical. He loudly announced his misfortune in being the blameless son of Alcmene and Zeus. Yet Hercules, who denounced Hera for hating him only because of his birth, at the same time hated Eurystheus for exactly the same reason. The two-months premature Eurystheus had not chosen to be born when or who he was.

Whether Hercules liked it or not, Eurystheus was king of Mycenae by right of birth and the proclamation of Zeus, and through no duplicity on his own part. He had not chosen his role, and was very much a pawn in a game much larger than himself. Without any wrongdoing on his part, the machinations of others had made Eurystheus the target of a hugely powerful, vindictive and homicidal hero. As Eurystheus pointed out, Hercules was not the only victim in this story - he had a pretty good claim to that status himself. Much later, he explained to Alcmene;

It was not I who chose to start this feud. Certainly, I was born cousin and kinsman to Heracles, your son. But this affliction was brought on me by the divine power of Hera, whether I wanted it or not. I never undertook to be his foe, and yet I had to enter into this struggle.

Naturally, I set myself to devise trouble in abundance. From time to time my midnight scheming bore fruit, as I learned how to push aside and slay my foes. And yes, I had to learn also to push aside fear of the future. That son of yours was not a nobody but a man indeed. Oh yes, he was my enemy, but I shall speak well of him, because he was a man of worth.
Eurystheus in *The Heracleidae* of Euripides l.986ff

And now Hercules was on his way to place himself in the service of Eurystheus. There was no need for Hera to point out how advantageous it would be for the king if his mighty rival died in the course of his duties. At one stroke, Eurystheus would become more secure on his throne. Nor would he have to dread that day when Hercules came and did the deed that, in his madness, he had already imagined doing.

The oracle had decreed that Hercules had to perform ten tasks for Eurystheus. One can imagine that a certain amount of midnight scheming was spent in the devising of these tasks. As we look at the Labours of Hercules over the coming chapters, we note certain points in common. One of these is that the tasks brought Eurystheus no personal gain. This is something to ponder upon. Why did Eurystheus not use Hercules as his personal battering ram against the armies and cities of his enemies? Or alternatively, why not send

Hercules to obtain precious stones and rare spices to fill his treasury? Yet Eurystheus set no such tasks. The Labours set for Hercules were either pointless or of benefit to humanity as a whole.

This tells us something about Eurystheus. He had been chosen as the arbiter and supervisor of the Labours of Hercules. The nature of the tasks chosen had to be difficult, bordering on impossible. Otherwise they would fail to meet the standard devised by Delphi, and indeed sought by Hercules himself in his vengeful quest for immortal glory.

At the same time Eurystheus had already a wary eye on the future and a time when (if) Hercules completed his appointed missions. At that point, Eurystheus became redundant to the needs of Hercules and the plans of the Gods. The only thing that might prevent him from being promptly slain by his former servant was if he could argue that he had completed the duty assigned to him fairly, impartially and without personal gain. Not that any such argument would impress Hercules, but it would work in the court of public opinion. Since one reason Hercules was doing the Labours was to boost his public image, it would only detract from the hero's glory if he unfairly killed the judge who was simply doing the job that Delphi and the Gods had ordered. So for Eurystheus, personal gain was out.

We also note something of a geographical progression to the Labours. The first six were all in the Peloponnese, because the kingdom of Eurystheus had indeed problems of a monstrous nature well suited to a herculean solution. Once these had been dealt with, Eurystheus devised missions which would take Hercules away from Mycenae, away from Greece, and to the very edges of the known world. Not only was there the hope that Hercules might encounter something insurmountably lethal on his travels, but the execution of each mission then became an end in itself. That is, it got Hercules far away from Eurystheus for as long as was superhumanly possible.

Another thing each Labour should accomplish was that it should directly or indirectly put Hercules on a collision course with one or more of the most fearsome creatures known in the world of myth. (And there were a fair few such creatures about.) On further reflection, we can see that Eurystheus extended this line of thought into a new direction, one based on the fact that some of the most fearful creatures known to mankind lived on top of Mount Olympus.

Hercules was not known for his tact or diplomatic skills. Hera already nursed a deadly hatred for Hercules. Perhaps some tasks could be assigned which would lead to Hercules upsetting other Gods, and so augmenting the divine anti-Hercules faction? This certainly involved a certain degree of mid-night scheming, because a task evidently designed to offend a god (e.g. 'Go and punch Apollo on the nose'), would rebound to the detriment of the task-setter rather than the executor.

What was needed were tasks that could be accomplished without incurring divine displeasure if they were executed with subtlety and finesse. If done with the brute force, mad-bull-at-a-gate style at which Hercules excelled, then it could be pointed out to a wrathful god that the fault lay not in the task, but in how it had been carried out. If all Hercules' Labours were of a type designed to upset someone divine and powerful, the Gods might become suspicious of Eurystheus, so moderation was the rule. Nevertheless, provo-king the wrath of one deity or another was the evident intent behind at least four of the Labours.

The First Labour – the Nemean Lion

This opening task of the assigned ten was by way of a warm-up. Hercules had merely to kill a monstrous lion and bring the pelt to Eurystheus. In later labours, Hercules would deal with creatures this fearsome as mere incidents along the way to fulfilling the primary task. For example, it will be seen that at one point Hercules ambushed and beat up Thanatos, Death himself, and that task was not even on the mission specification. So dealing with a man-eating lion was indeed a gentle warm-up for the Labours. Especially as Hercules already had a decent track record in that department, as the grateful inhabitants of Cythairon mountain range could testify.

Admittedly, this particular lion was a substantial step up from Hercules' earlier effort. The beast was no ordinary carnivore, but a child of Typhon and Echidna. To put the Lion in perspective, a quick introduction to the parents is necessary. Typhon was one of those proto-monsters who had almost managed to destroy the cosmos. He was said to stand 'half as high as the stars' and had a hundred dragon's heads where the normal human cranium would be. Zeus had attempted to go one-on-one with Typhon and had been soundly defeated. In the end it took the combined efforts of all the Gods to bring Typhon under control, and even then Team Olympus almost lost the battle. Though the Typhonian menace had ultimately been contained, any child of the super-monster deserved more than a modicum of respect. As for Echidna, the Lion's mother was known as the 'mother of monsters', and with such to be described, no-one does the job better than Hesiod.

Ferocious Echidna, the Goddess. She is half a nymph with fair cheeks and a shy glance - and half a huge and awesome snake with speckled skin. Within the sacred earth she gnaws on raw flesh in a deep-hollowed cave within the rock. She has been granted this glorious dwelling here, far from the immortal Gods and mortal humanity. In Arima, she keeps guard beneath the earth. Grim Echidna, the nymph who neither dies nor grows old through all her days.
Hesiod *Theogony* 295-305

This lion child of the two awful creatures, Typhon and Echnida, was suckled and raised on the moon before falling from the bosom of Selene to make his home in Nemea, in the Peloponnese not far from Mycenae. The town of Nemea was later famous for its games, which were seen as in the same class as the Pythian, Delphic and Olympic Games, for a temple of Zeus (parts of which still stand today), and of course, for its Lion.

That the Argolid region, which included Nemea, should be afflicted by this monster was remarkable. The Argolid came under the special protection of Hera, and yet it was Hera who had unleashed the Lion upon the very people whom she was meant to defend. One suggestion is that Hera liked to bathe in a sacred spring near Argos every year – a process which renewed her virginity and so made her more fascinating to her over-sexed spouse. Believing that she had been spied upon during a recent bathing excursion, Hera had retaliated violently.

The quick-tempered wife of Zeus set him [the Nemean Lion] *loose to damage Argos.*
Callimachus *Aetia Fragment* 55

The Lion, like its Cytheronian counterpart, busily set about depopulating the flocks and herds in the area. It also acquired the habit of abducting and killing young women. When local heroes set out to rescue each woman, the Lion would lurk in the recesses of the cave pretending to be its victim.

When the unsuspecting rescuers came within range, the Lion would revert to its true shape and rend the heroes tooth and claw. As a punishment to the people of Nemea, the Lion was both painful and effective. No doubt delegations came to Eurystheus pointing out that, as taxpayers, the local people expected action from their ruler on this matter. So we can see why Eurystheus made getting rid of the Lion a priority. What is surprising was that Hera let him do this.

Since Eurystheus was working hand-in-glove with the Goddess, it is unlikely that he would have Hercules kill this Lion without Hera's consent. But perhaps that consent had been given. After all, it was one thing to unleash a monster upon the countryside in a fit of pique; it was quite another thing for that monster to keep ravaging the land and making its protectors look bad.

Since those protectors were King Eurystheus and patron goddess Hera respectively, perhaps it was now time for the Lion to go. Of course there was no guarantee that Hercules would not fall at the first hurdle, and instead of Hercules disposing of the Lion, the Lion might dispose of Hercules. In fact that was the beauty of this first Labour. However things worked out, the result would be a win for Eurystheus and Hera. The perfect outcome would be for one protagonist to be mortally wounded in the process of killing the other. Unlikely, but one could always hope.

So Hercules was sent on his way. In comparison to the later missions which took him over much of the known world and beyond, the trip to Nemea barely constituted a day's journey for Hercules. His destination was nearby in the mountains, a narrow pass with a cave on the side.

The pass is called Tretos ['Pierced']. *It is narrow, for the mountains press close on all sides ... . Here in these mountains they still point out the cave of the famous Lion, some fifteen stades* [2.3 km] *distant from Nemea itself.*
Pausanias *Guide to Greece* 2. 15. 2

What happened next we can hear from Hercules himself, as he told it to a man called Phyleus. The tale was preserved by the poet Theocritus who recorded it in his bucolic *Idylls* (25.132ff) in the third century BC.

Phyleus to Hercules:

'An Achaean came from Archaea, from Helix by the sea. He told me that he had witnessed the slaying of that creature, the dreadful scourge of the countryside, the monstrous lion which has its lair by the grove sacred to Zeus of Nemea. The slaying was done by an Argive, and I believe that man was yourself, for the lion skin draped over your sides confirms that this epic deed was done by your hand.'

' I am certain that so huge a monster would never be found in all of Apis, which supports only bears and boars. So tell of how this affliction came to well-watered Nemea, and how you slew it with your bare hands.'

Hercules to Phyleus:

'Since you ask, I can tell you everything about this monster apart from whence it came. For that matter, no Argive knows this - even though some make that claim. The best guess is that one of the sacred Gods was angry with the sons of Phoroneus [a primordial king of the Peloponnese whose mother was – surprise, surprise – raped by Zeus]. *So the scourge of the Lion was unleashed, and like a river bursting into a valley it devastated all in its path. The people of Bembiana suffered more of the pitiless onslaught than they could endure, so Eurystheus laid on me this first Labour to complete. I had to kill this ferocious beast.'*

'So I set out, taking with me my supple bow and hollow quiver filled with arrows ... . When I arrived at the Lion's hunting grounds, I took my bow. I fitted the string to the curved horns and aligned it with my grief-bringing arrows. Then it was a matter of scouting for the accursed monster and locating him before he discovered me. ... I had neither sight of his tracks or sound of his roar, but still the pallor of fear hung over the farmsteads. It was the middle of the day, yet no man worked with his oxen or laboured in the fields; there was no-one who could give me directions. So without a pause I headed for the leafy mountainside and searched. When the Lion was found, I would immediately test my strength on him.'

'Immediately' did not happen that day, nor the next. For weeks Hercules searched in vain, for it seemed he was fated to be exactly where the Lion was not. Even though the Lion was unaware of the hunter, time and again the whims of chance took him out of one side of the pass just as Hercules entered from the other side. Then after the Lion had circled his hunting grounds he would again enter the pass and his cave just as Hercules left via the other exit. This went on for almost a month, and the exasperated hero realized that it could continue indefinitely. So, as was his wont, he took drastic steps to change the situation. A few hours later, the narrow mountain pass was no more. A Hercules-induced rock-slide had completely closed off one end of the pass. At the other end our hero lurked in the bushes with bow in hand and killing in mind. Now Hercules takes up the tale again:

'It was late in the day when the Lion returned to his lair. His tongue licked his chops, for he had feasted on meat and blood. The evidence was splattered over his squalid mane, his glaring face and his chest. On that woodland path I had been waiting for him, hiding in the shadow of some bushes. Now as he passed, I let loose a swift arrow at his flank – and failed. '

'I expected the arrow to run true between the ridges [of the lion's ribs] *but instead it bounced off and fell useless to the green grass. Astonished, the Lion snarled wickedly through his teeth and raised his great head higher from the ground, searching all around with his keen gaze. Angry at wasting my first shot, I let a second loose from the string, and this time scored a hit right in the chest, at the very seat of the lungs. The arrow, which should have inflicted agony, hit the hide and then dropped between his paws, as useless as the one before. In furious disgust I prepared to draw for the third time.'*

'But the rolling eyes of the monstrous beast had settled upon me, and the lion prepared himself for battle. His tail lashed his thighs, his throat swelled with fury, and anger bristled his tawny mane. Raging to taste my flesh, he arched his spine like a bow, gathering his length between flanks and midriff. Then the terrible creature sprang from afar to right upon me in a moment. I had taken my cloak from my shoulders and folded it with the arrows in one hand [as a makeshift shield]. *In my other hand I held my seasoned club of*

wild olive. Now I swung that club back past my ears and smashed it down on his skull. Tough as it was, the wood splintered to pieces on the invincible monster's maned skull. But it dropped the brute before he could reach me, and he fell, landing on shaky feet and swinging his head from side to side to clear the darkness that rose behind his eyes from the stunning impact ... .'

'Seeing him stunned and confused with pain, I moved in quickly before he could regain his wits and his breath. Throwing bow and embroidered quiver to the ground, I grabbed the beast by the scruff of his iron neck. Then with all the strength in my hands I began to strangle him. It was necessary to do this from behind lest his claws eviscerate my body, so I pinned his hind feet to the ground with my heels while my knees squeezed his flanks. Then with my hands [around the Lion's neck] *I stretched the body out. Finally it collapsed asphyxiated into my arms, and Hades, Lord of the Underworld, received the Lion's spirit.'*

Hercules had won. He had killed the Lion, but he had not yet completed his Labour. That Labour was to bring to Eurystheus the skin of the mighty Lion. And there Hercules hit a problem. His arrows had bounced off the Lion's hide because the Lion had two remarkable attributes - claws which could rip through anything (hence Hercules' care to keep out of their way) and an impenetrable hide. This left Hercules with a conundrum. How does one remove the pelt from a beast that can't be skinned? First Hercules tried with a knife, just to confirm what the arrows had already demonstrated. Making no impression with the blade, he tried sharpening the knife on a stone. Finally he smashed the stone, and tried cutting the hide with the sharp edges. When even that failed, our hero was stumped.

Fortunately, Hercules was seldom alone in his labours. As usual, Athena was watching over her protégé, and Athena was definitely the brains of the outfit. The Goddess gently pointed out to the perplexed hero that an impenetrable hide could not co-exist in the same universe with claws which could rip through anything. Either the claws were an irresistible force or the hide was an immovable object - but when the Lion's claws were applied to the Lion's hide, something had to give.

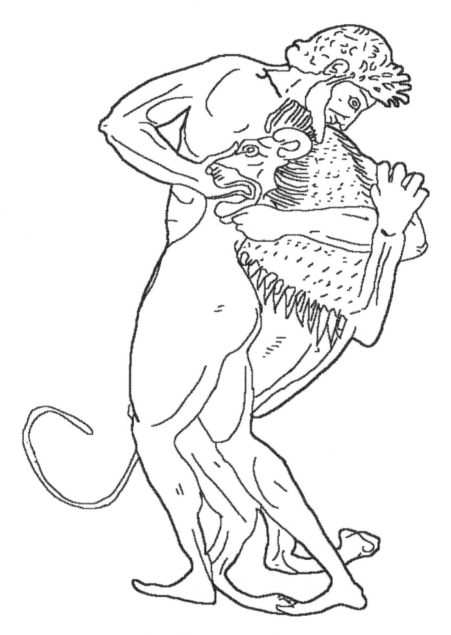

Unbeatable Hero v. Invincible lion
From a black-figure wine jug c.510 BC from Etruria and now in the British Museum

When the matter was put to the test, the claws won the day. Hercules finally had the means to slice through the monster's skin and remove the pelt. This he did with some care. It had occurred to him (or more probably it had occurred to Athena who passed along the idea) that Eurystheus had stipulated that Hercules must bring the Lion's skin to him. This Hercules would do, and no more than that. Having brought the skin to Eurystheus, the Labour was complete.

After presenting the pelt for inspection, Hercules had no intention of giving it up. The hide was much more than a trophy to commemorate the successful completion of the First Labour. Cut properly from its previous owner, the invulnerable lion-skin could be fashioned into a cloak. Given the perils that lay in Hercules' future, a garment totally impervious to sharp objects was a very welcome addition to his wardrobe.

As Hercules concludes,

'There, my friend, you have that tale of the doom of the Lion of Nemea, that creature which brought so many sorrows to flocks and to men.'
Theocritus *Idylls* 25.280

This is not quite the end of the tale. On his way to confront the Lion, Hercules had been the guest of a peasant farmer called Molorchus. The farmer was planning to sacrifice a ram to Zeus Soter (Zeus the Saviour). Hercules persuaded the man to wait for thirty days. If he returned within that period, the pair would sacrifice to Zeus together in thanks for his salvation. If Hercules failed to return, then Molorchus would sacrifice anyway, but this time to the spirit of the dead hero.

The sacrifice was already prepared, and the ram about to be killed in Hercules' name when the proposed honorand arrived in the nick of time. Though the sacrifice went ahead, dedicated to Zeus, Hercules had a small funeral of his own to arrange. Through pride or stoicism he had failed to mention to Phyleus that the strangulation of the Lion had not gone as smoothly as might be wished. At some point the beast had managed to chew off one of Hercules' fingers.

Heracles had only nine fingers after the Nemean Lion had bitten off one. There exists a tomb for this detached finger ... one can see it at Sparta. There is a stone lion erected on the tomb to symbolize of the power of the hero. Thus began the tradition of placing stone lions on the tombs of distinguished people. Ptolemy Hephaestion, *New History* 2

The Nemean Lion has a memorial of his own, and one befitting so mighty a beast. From July to August the Lion rules the cosmos as the astrological sign of Leo. The constellation crouches in the sky between Cancer in the west and Virgo to the east. Perhaps the Lion dreams of the distant future when the slow drift of the galaxy brings the constellation of Hercules within his reach, and the pair can square off for a celestial re-match.

Chapter 5

Hero at work

Hercules presented himself at the court of Eurystheus and there showed the king evidence of the successful completion of his first mission. The sight of Hercules standing before him, armed and invulnerable in his lion-skin cloak, caused a certain degree of introspection in the already insecure monarch. In future, he decreed, there was no need for Hercules to present his grisly proofs in person. The matter could be settled by a panel of judges outside the city gates without Eurystheus needing to actually meet his dangerous relative. Just in case Hercules disregarded these instructions, Eurystheus ordered the construction of a large bronze urn. This was buried up to the neck in the throne room, and had a lid designed to withstand extreme pressure. Then, in the hope that the world's first panic room would be ready before Hercules returned, Eurystheus sent the hero off on his second mission.

This Labour continued Eurystheus' vendetta with the children of Typhon and snake-bodied Echidna. This time the child in question took after her mother. Echidna's lower body was that of a monstrous serpent, but the Lernean Hydra went one better and had not only the lower body of a serpent but the upper part as well. Unlike the Nemean Lion, which was already plaguing the Argolid before the Labours were thought of, the Hydra had been carefully prepared for the forthcoming challenge like a star athlete before a major event.

...the evil-minded Hydra of Lerna was nourished by white-armed Hera, for the goddess was beyond furious with mighty Heracles.
Hesiod *Theogony* 313

The Hydra was the most lethally poisonous creature in creation. Lesser serpents might kill men with their bite, but the Hydra could do so with just her breath. In fact, the writer Hyginus assures us that so venomous was the creature that any man who so much as breathed in deeply while he crossed the path where the monster had slithered 'died in the greatest torment' (*Fabulae* 30).

Unsurprisingly, locals were deeply distressed by the arrival of this monstrous creature. Distressed, but not necessarily surprised. The town was already unhealthy, as it was situated beside a marsh. Into that marsh every year a lamb was cast as a sacrifice to the beings which lay beneath its waters, for Lerna was one of the few places where the Underworld of Hades was linked directly to the world of men. In fact it may have been around the time of the arrival of the Hydra that Lerna was abandoned altogether - modern archaeological excavations of the site date the abandonment to the later Bronze Age - and thereafter the place was used as a graveyard by the people of Argos, presumably to save the deceased from a lengthy journey to Hades.

Distant from Argos forty stades [four miles] *and no more is the sea at Lerna. On the way to Lerna the first thing on the road is the Erasinus spring, which empties into the Phrixus river, and the Phrixus meets the sea between Temenium and Lerna.*
Pausanias *Guide to Greece* 2.36.6

Where the 'torpid stream' of another spring left the marsh was a hillock on which grew a large tree. This spring was the Amymone, named after a distant ancestor of Hercules. In Roman times the tree was seen by the peripatetic Pausanias during the preparation of his *Guide to Greece*, though by his time a certain scepticism had crept in.

At the source of the Amymone grows a plane tree. They say it was in the shadow of this tree that the Hydra came into its strength. I am ready to believe that this creature was larger that other water-snakes, and that its poison was exceptionally deadly ... . However, I believe it had originally one head and not many. It was first described as multi-headed by Peisander of Kamiros, who did it to make the monster more terrifying and his poem more memorable.
Pausanias, *Guide to Greece* 2.37.4

The Hydra's den was under this tree in the swamp. From this base the monster made regular sallies into the surrounding countryside where it devastated crops and herds of cattle. So again Eurystheus would have been duty-bound to send a hero to destroy the creature, even if Hera did not already have the confrontation in mind. Furthermore, as with the Nemean Lion, Hercules had previous experience in this brand of monster slaying. As the first century AD playwright and philosopher Seneca remarked - perhaps not altogether seriously - when the two serpents sent by Hera (p.11) 'had their swollen throats crushed by his [Hercules'] baby hands, he was practising for the Hydra.' (*Hercules Furens* 220ff)

Pausanias may also have been correct that the Hydra started its career as the bane of Argos with just a single head, but Hera had built in a nasty surprise for Hercules or any other hero who came to destroy the monster. Traditionally the way to kill a snake was to chop off its head, so Hera arranged that as soon as a head was lopped off, another two would spring up in its place.

(This is why the Hydra became the symbol of the SLA terrorist group in the 1970s and the name of the subversive organization in the Marvel comic books. Destroy one branch and two others were supposed to spring up in its place. Today a 'hydra-headed' problem is a situation where any solution just makes things worse.)

Since the Hydra had nine heads by the time Hercules got around to it, we can assume that at least one hero had made the attempt to deal with the beast already. The longest continuous account of the meeting of Hercules and Hydra comes from the *Library* of Apollodorus, and to this we now turn:

For his second Labour Eurystheus ordered Heracles to kill the Lernean Hydra. Born of the Lernean marsh, that monster would go out to the plain and there ravage both the cattle and the country. The Hydra had an immense body and nine heads. Eight of these were mortal, but the middle one was indestructible. [By some accounts the middle head was of gold]

So Heracles mounted his chariot and with Iolaus his charioteer, he came to Lerna. The horses were halted when the Hydra was discovered on the hill beside the springs of the Amymone, where it had its den. Into that den Heracles unleashed a storm of fire arrows, and so forced the monster to emerge.

Antonio del Pollaiolo (1431-1498) *Ercole e l'Idra.* Galleria degli Uffizi, Florence

As soon as it did so he seized it and held on tightly.

The battle began. Hercules had protected himself from the snake's venomous breath by winding a wet scarf about his face, and the Hydra now reciprocated by winding itself around Hercules' body. At this point another of Hera's little surprises popped up.

While the Hydra wound itself about one of his feet and clung to him, a huge crab now came to the aid of the Hydra by sinking its pincers into Heracles' foot.

Hercules smashed the crab to pieces with his club, but was stumped by the obstinate refusal of the Hydra's heads to be stumped. Being Hercules, our hero obstinately continued decapitating the beast until a veritable forest of heads now confronted him, each with venom dripping from its fangs. Things looked grim for our hero until a bolt of inspiration hit him.

As the crab had helped the Hydra, in his turn he called on Iolaus who set fire to part of a nearby wood and heated his sword in the flames. Then as Heracles took off each head, he cauterized the stump and so stopped new heads from sprouting. Having dealt with the multiplying heads, he [Hercules] *then chopped off the immortal one.*
Apollodorus *Library* 2.5.2

In his epic poem *The Fall of Troy* the Roman poet Quintus Smyrnaeus pictured the scene.

The many-necked Hydra flickered its dreadful tongues. Some of its fearsome heads lay severed on the earth, but many more were budding from its necks. That stout-hearted pair, Hercules and Iolaos, were hard at their toil. The one mowed off the fierce heads with mighty strokes, while his companion seared each neck with glowing iron until the monster was slain.

The cunning idea of cauterizing the Hydra's necks is specifically attributed by most authors to the inspiration of Athena. Hesiod, for example bluntly states that the creature was destroyed 'by the plan of Athena' (*Theogony* 313).

However, we do not know whether it was through the suggestion of the Goddess or by his own initiative that Hercules slit open the poison sac of the snake, and dipped the heads of his arrows within. The arrowheads absorbed the venom and became almost as deadly as the snake itself. In his case, what did not kill him certainly made Hercules stronger - he now had an incomparably deadly weapon to go with the invulnerable shield of the Nemean Lion's skin. Hercules was fond of calling his arrows 'sorrow-bringing'. He could not have known how accurate that description would later prove to be.

The final, immortal head had been the last to be chopped off. This Hercules buried on his way home at the roadside on the way to Elaeus. To make sure that no-one unearthed the head - which, being immortal, would be both alive and in a foul mood when found - he placed a large rock over the burial site. The rest of the corpse was burned in the impromptu pyre that the cauterizing fire had created. Thereafter the waters of the marsh were hot, pungent and undrinkable. Given the marsh's pre-existing link to the Underworld, one might suspect a sulphuric volcanic spring, but the ancients had other ideas

The marsh of Lerna where the burnt Hydra's heat makes warm the depths of those polluted waters
Statius, *Thebaid* 2.375

Death simply shifted the Hydra to the other side of the portals of the Underworld. The monstrous snake remained as a guard barring entry to the Kingdom of Hades, a job which it shared with that better known custodian, Cerberus - a hound also bountifully-endowed in cranial development. Although the crab sent by Hera was, (almost literally) a footnote in the story, the creature was rewarded for its kamikaze ankle-biting attack with a place in the heavens next to Leo where it became the astrological sign of Cancer.

The Cerynitian Hind

The capture of the Cerynitian Hind was to be Hercules' second Labour. Those of an arithmetical inclination might object to this designation, as the Labours of the Nemean Lion and the Lernean Hydra already made two, and the Hind

59

should therefore be counted as the third. However, Eurystheus ruled a technical foul on the Lernean Hydra. This was because Hercules had not done the job alone. Iolaus had helped by cauterizing the Hydra's necks before more heads could sprout, and had therefore played an essential part in the creature's destruction. Since these were The Labours of Hercules and not The Labours of Hercules and Assistant, Eurystheus ruled that the second Labour would have to be done again.

We now get some indication of how much research Hercules put into his quarry each time a Labour was announced. Certainly our hero would benefit from investigating the background, the strengths and potential weaknesses of each creature he was sent out against, and for this next Labour such a check was particularly important. Hercules would have discovered that the Cerynitian Hind was unusual among female deer in that it had antlers. Nor were these normal antlers, but shining horns of purest gold. The Hind was one of a group of five deer. All of them were spectacularly fast runners, but this one was the speediest of all. (For which reason in the Elizabethan era England's great sailor Sir Francis Drake called his ship *The Golden Hind*).

This super-deer could leap tall buildings and run faster than a speeding arrow. It too was a problem for agriculture in the Peloponnese for the late Roman poet Quintus Smyrnaeus informs us that it 'laid waste the vineyards of hapless husbandmen ... with its golden horns and breath of ravening fire.' (*Fall of Troy* 6. 223) Seven hundred years before Quintus Smyrnaeus, the poet Callimachus supplied the further information that the group of deer to which the Hind belonged were 'larger than bulls' (*3rd Hymn to Artemis* 98 ff).

Given these attributes it is perhaps unsurprising that Eurystheus made the labour of catching the animal even more difficult by stipulating that the beast should be brought to him unharmed. The surprise is that Eurystheus intended to keep the Hind imprisoned once it had been captured. Certainly it would be a very bad idea to have the animal killed, and this is where Hercules' background check would have paid off. Here is the gist of that research.

It begins at Mt Tagetus, the formidable mountain which looms over the little town of Sparta in modern Greece. In ancient times it was on the slopes of this mountain that the Spartans would expose their new-born children in a scientific spirit of enquiry as to whether they were tough enough to survive the night. Those who did survive might have been aided in their struggle for survival by the nymph Taygete, denizen of that mountain and mother of

Lacedaemon, the founder of the Spartan race. Like many a nymph in those distant days, Taygete had problems coping with the amorous advances of Zeus. Offending the King of the Gods by refusing him was almost as dangerous as offending his wife by not refusing him, so one can understand Taygete's gratitude at being helped out of her perilous predicament by the hunter-goddess Artemis. Artemis turned Taygete into a cow until Zeus turned his affections elsewhere, and in return for this favour Tagete gave five golden-horned deer to the Goddess.

Five were there in all, and four you [Artemis] *captured by speed of foot alone, with no hounds to aid you in the chase. They were tasked to draw your swift chariot, and to that golden chariot did you yoke them, and golden bridles, Goddess, you put on your deer.*

But one deer was too swift and escaped over the river Celadon, and the hills of Ceryneia received her ... .(Callimachus *ibid*)

The deer which escaped became the favourite of Artemis, perhaps because according to the poet Pindar (522–443 BC) the hind was in fact Tagete herself. With her deer companion for company Artemis hunted among the hills around Ceryneia - in those days one of the twelve great Achaean cities. Today, in the modern era, it is a village with a population of five hundred.

Given this background, one can see that Artemis might be somewhat miffed if her deer was taken away from her, but positively annoyed if her companion was hurt or even killed in the taking. Like her twin brother Apollo, Artemis had a wide vindictive streak running through her character.

Her mother, Leto, had trouble giving birth to Apollo and Artemis, as she was cursed not to give birth on land or sea and so was constantly refused a place to deliver her children. The pair were eventually born on the sacred isle of Delos. Once they had grown up, Artemis and Apollo methodically hunted down and killed all who had refused their pregnant mother shelter elsewhere. Later there was Niobe, queen of Thebes, who boasted that she had fourteen children while Leto had but two. Those two children of Leto took umbrage at Niobe's attitude, promptly took up their bows, and slaughtered the queen's children until she also had only a pair remaining.

Chione, princess of Phocis was killed because she claimed to be prettier than

Artemis, and the handsome Adonis got the chop for claiming to be a better hunter. (Presumably the pork chop, as Artemis had him killed by a wild boar.) The hunter Actaeon was turned into a stag and torn apart by his own hounds because he glimpsed Artemis bathing nude, and Aura, goddess of the breeze, was raped and driven insane for doubting Artemis' virginity. Then there was the unfortunate Callisto, the late Orion and ... but you get the picture.

Under the circumstances Eurystheus was being pretty heroic in ordering Hercules to capture the pet of Artemis, and positively deranged if he thought he could keep it. However, the wily king was probably correct in his assumption that the goddesses' wrath would fall primarily on Hercules. Just as Hercules assumed the guilt for killing his children even though he had been the unwitting agent of Hera and Lyssa, so Hercules would be guilty of capturing Artemis' companion. In the opinion of Artemis and her contemporaries it would matter far less who ordered Hercules to do the deed than that Hercules actually did it. In the Heroic Age, a man was seriously responsible for his own actions.

So while the previous tasks had involved killing dangerous creatures, in this case Hercules had to capture a dangerous and elusive creature alive - and in the process avoid something far more dangerous, the wrath of Olympian Artemis. Off to Arcadia went our hero, and there he spent an educational year chasing through the glens and mountains while learning of the hundreds of ways that the Hind could not be caught. After all, this was a beast that even the Goddess of the Hunt had failed to capture, and Hercules' task was further complicated by his earnest desire not to harm a hair on the creature's lovely hide.

From Oinoe to Mt Artemision the chase entertained the people of Arcadia from week to week 'over mountain haunts to untrodden meadows, through groves where flocks graze,' says the poet Aelian (*Animalia* 7.39). That Mt Artemision was the Hind's final shelter is revealing, for the mountain was sacred to Artemis. Indeed, in later years any sanctuary to the goddess was called an Artemision, including that temple at Ephesus which became one of the Seven Wonders of the World.

Doggedly Hercules pressed his pursuit even here, and forced his weary quarry to flee again. The Hind attempted to ford the Ladon river which flowed - and still flows - at the base of the mountain and on into the Ionian sea.

Hercules Behind the Hind
Sketch from a 6th century Black figure vase in the British Museum

Here, at the place where Demeter had washed away the shame of being raped by Poseidon, Hercules saw his chance. The waters of the river were not deep, but fast waters run shallow, and the Hind struggled in the crossing. Hercules, the consummate archer, carefully selected an arrow not tipped with the Hydra's lethal poison and shot it at the Hind. As planned, the arrow went not into the creature but between its forelegs. This caused it to stumble into the water - and by some accounts to dent one of its golden horns in the process.

In a flash, Hercules was on his prey, and slinging the captured beast over his shoulders, he set out for Mycenae.

Inevitably, the journey home brought Hercules into contact with the one person he least wished to meet; Artemis, out for a stroll. Just to make things worse, she was accompanied by her equally vindictive twin brother Apollo. Fortunately for Hercules, he had a few things going in his favour. Firstly the Hind had suffered no permanent damage. Secondly, as Adonis and Orion could have testified (before their unfortunate demise), virgin or no, Artemis had an eye for a well-set young man. Finally, Hercules was a protégé of Athena and no-one in their right mind offended Athena, be they ploughman or Olympian god. So, calling on powers of oratory he never knew he possessed, our hero pitched his case to the offended Artemis. He put the blame for the capture on Eurystheus and Hera, and appealed for sympathy through the circumstances that had forced him to perform the labours. It helped that Hera and Artemis did not particularly get along, as shown in a later incident.

As Hera spoke, she caught both of Artemis' arms at the wrists and boxed her ears as Artemis tried to twist away, so her arrows flew [from their quiver] *and were scattered. Artemis got free and fled in tears, as a pigeon from a hawk.* Homer, *Iliad* 21.475

So Artemis was not above sabotaging the plans of her step-mother, and allowed herself to be persuaded to let Hercules go on his way, extracting from him only the promise that the Hind should be returned unharmed at the completion of his Labour.

Heracles thus soothed the goddess' wrath; and brought the animal still living to Mycenae Apollodorus, *Library* 2.81

This left Hercules with one remaining problem. He had promised to deliver the Hind to Eurystheus for his menagerie, and at the same time had promised Artemis he would set the Hind free. Not delivering the Hind to Eurystheus would mean another Labour disqualified, just as the killing of the Hydra had been. On the other hand, delivering the Hind as ordered would break a solemn promise given personally to Artemis. Neither prospect was appealing, and Hercules doubtless spent the remainder of his journey to Mycenae pondering this conundrum.

As already arranged, Hercules was to present proof of the completion of his Labours to a panel of judges at the city gates. However, our hero insisted that as a point of order, he could not do so on this occasion. He was ordered to deliver the Hind to Eurystheus, and no-one but Eurystheus, and the Labour would not be complete until the delivery was done personally. Hercules was insistent that this Labour was not going to be disqualified on a technicality. Since the Hind was relatively harmless in comparison to Hercules' usual quarry, Eurystheus cautiously agreed to the terms. When the king arrived at the city gates, Hercules ostentatiously presented the Hind to him, setting the animal down at the king's feet.

As soon as Hercules released his grip, the Hind demonstrated its famous speed. It took off from a standing start, and briefly became a golden streak that vanished in the direction of Arcadia. While this development left king and courtiers nonplussed, Hercules merely shrugged. He had followed his orders to the letter, and delivered the Hind to Eurystheus. That Eurystheus had proven incapable of maintaining custody for more than a split second was a problem, but not Hercules' problem. He had kept his promises to both Eurystheus and Artemis. His Labour was complete.

Chapter 6

Sidetracks on the path to glory

Centaurs were once common creatures in the world of mythology. Like the satyrs and harpies, they were liminal creatures, caught somewhere between beast and man, nature and supernature. The common centaur had the rationality of a human, but used that rationality to gratify a nature which was coarse, bestial and savage.

The centaurs could hardly be blamed for this, given the circumstances by which their species had come about. The ancestor of the centaurs was Ixion, king of the Lapith tribe and a son of Ares the war-god. Ixion came to Mt Olympus in questionable circumstances, and thereafter tried to rape his grand-mother, Hera. However, the suspicious Zeus already suspected Ixion, and had anticipated his crime. Therefore he shaped a cloud into the form of Hera, and Ixion had his way with that.

Ixion duly received a ghastly punishment, while the cloud retained its form to become the goddess Nephele who gave birth to a deformed child called Centaurus. Centaurus possessed his father's undisciplined sexuality, but lacked even his father's discrimination. Shunning human company, Centaurus lived in the wilderness about Mt Pelion in Thessaly, and mated with the wild mares which lived thereabouts.

Thus arose 'the cloud-born Centaurs' (as the Roman poet Vergil puts it in his *Aeneid*). These were powerful creatures who feuded frequently with their human blood-relatives in Ixion's Lapith tribe. The centaurs had come second in the most recent bout of blood-letting, and by the time of Hercules they were taking refuge in the mountains of Arcadia. Among the refugees lived a different type of centaur. This was Pholus. While most centaurs were mostly horse with a human growing from the waist where a horse's neck would be, Pholus was a human with a horse's hindquarters growing from his buttocks, rather like a pantomime pony before the front man has put on his costume.

It was necessary for the mythologisers to explain this distinction, because in later ages centaurs of all types were extinct. For those in the audience who wanted to know what had happened to the centaurs, the answer is basically 'Hercules'. While Hercules was to slaughter individual survivors later and under different circumstances, the main massacre happened while the hero was on his way to perform his fourth Labour. (Or his third, according to Eurystheus.)

The object of this Labour was to capture alive a massive boar which was terrorizing north-western Arcadia. (It will be noted that Hercules' labours were already taking him farther afield. Mt Artemesion, where Hercules had captured the Cerynitian Hind lay right on the border of the Argolid, while the present mission would take our hero right across Arcadia to the borders of Achaea.)

Since Hercules had taken a year to complete his previous task, he was inclined to pace himself with this more distant Labour. Knowing that the home of the learned centaur Pholus lay on his route just south of Mt Erymanthos where the boar dwelled, Hercules dropped in to break bread and partake of the creature's hospitality. In fact not bread but a specimen of the local wildlife was broken open, for Pholus was enough of a centaur to prefer his meet raw. However the other half of dinner was roasted in deference to Hercules' more human tastes. All that was required for a fully convivial meal was a beaker of wine, so Hercules asked his host if he had any to share.

At this point the writers Apollodorus (*Library* 2.5.4ff) and Diodorus Siculus (*History* 4.12.3ff) take up the tale.

There was wine, but it had been buried in the earth. As the writers of myth tell us, four generations previously this wine had been given to Centaurus by Dionysus [the god of wine] *himself.* (Diodorus)

When Heracles called for wine, Pholus said he was afraid to open this jar which belonged not to him, but to the Centaurs as a tribe. Heracles cheerfully told Pholus not to worry, and opened the wine anyway. (Apollodorus)

Now this wine was of great age and potency. When the jar was opened, the sweet odour drifted to the centaurs who lived around, and drove them mad. Consequently, they formed a terrifying mob and rushed to the cave of Pholus intent on plundering the wine from him. (Diodorus)

While Pholus took cover, Heracles struggled with these beings which had the strength of two creatures combined with the wisdom and experience of men. Some were armed with pine trees, pulled up by the roots. Others hurled huge rocks, and still others were armed with flaming torches and the large axes used to slaughter oxen. The centaurs were aided by their mother Nephele who let loose a deluge of rain, which little troubled those with the stability of four legs, but made things very slippery for he who supported himself on two. Yet despite disadvantages such as these, Heracles showed no signs of fear, but fought in a manner worthy of his former exploits. (Diodorus)

The first who dared enter were repelled by Heracles with a shower of flame from the fire. The rest he shot, and then pursued the survivors as far as Malea. (Apollodorus)

This was no brief chase in the heat of the moment, but a long, vindictive hunt. Pholus had hosted his ill-advised dinner party close to the home of the boar Hercules was ordered to capture. This animal lived on Mt Erymanthos in the north-west of Arcadia. Malea, to where the surviving centaurs fled, is some 138km (86 miles) away on the other side of the Peloponnese as far to the south-east as one can get without running into the sea.

Some centaurs scattered away from the main body of refugees, some ending at Eleusis, where they were given sanctuary by Poseidon, and others to live solitary lives as exiles (Hercules tended to kill these latter refugees whenever he came across them). However, the flight of most of the centaurs to Malea was not merely intended to take them as far from Hercules as it was equinely possible to get. Their hope of safety lay with Cheiron, who had made his home on that mountainous promontory.

Cheiron was 'the wisest and most just of the centaurs', says Homer (*Iliad* 11.831). He was of different birth to the other centaurs, being a child of the elder gods. Noble and immortal, he had been instructed in the arts of music, medicine and prophecy by Apollo and Artemis, and his arcane abilities evidently also extended into the dimensions of time. We know this because he

Hercules Making centaurs extinct
Statue by Giambologna (1529 – 1608) Loggia dei Lanze, Florence Italy.

is firmly attested as the instructor of Achilles, a lad whose birth lay a generation after Cheiron's unfortunate demise. Cheiron was also known to be a friend of Hercules, and this is probably why the centaurs fled to him in the hope the he would intercede with their grim pursuer.

As the centaurs cowered about Cheiron, Heracles shot an arrow at them. This passed through the arm of [the centaur called] *Elatus, and continued to finally impale itself in the knee of Cheiron. Distressed by this development, Heracles ran up and pulled out the shaft. Then he applied a medicine which Cheiron supplied to him. But the wound was incurable. Cheiron withdrew into his cave. There he intended to die, but could not, for he was immortal.*
(Apollodorus)

The problem lay with the virulently destructive poison of the Hydra. The arrows which Hercules had spiked with this lethal venom brought certain death to all whom they touched. Therefore Cheiron hovered in agony; ever about to die, yet constantly pulled back from the brink of death by his immortality.

Eventually the noble Prometheus offered to take on himself Cheiron's immortality and the accompanying agony. This was all the more self-sacrificing as Prometheus had problems of his own. Punished by Zeus for giving fire to mankind, he had spent the last eon or two chained to a rock atop a mountain in the Caucasus range, awaiting the eagle which came every day to feast on his liver. Taking on Cheiron's pain along with his own was an additional burden, but it proved a good investment. Hercules remembered the favour, and as will be seen, eventually more than repaid it.

Thus died Cheiron, neither the first nor the last to perish from knowing Hercules. The next to discover that the hero's company was more dangerous than a roomful of infuriated vipers was Pholus, the centaur whose misplaced sense of hospitality had been the death of his kind. Pholus had been disconsolately tracking the trail of slain centaurs towards Malea and burying the corpses as he went along. Puzzled as to how the sturdy centaurs had been felled by relatively trivial wounds, Pholus extracted an arrow. As he studied it thoughtfully, the blood-slick shaft slipped from his fingers and fell to impale him in the foot. Hercules returned to find Pholus dead on the spot.

He gave him a magnificent funeral and buried him at the base of the mountain.
This preserves his reputation better than any gravestone. For Mt Pholos now
bears his name and all know who is buried there without needing an
inscription.
(Apollodorus)

Hercules now went on to perform his duty and capture the Erymanthian Boar.
However, this *Parergus* (minor event accompanying the Labours) with the
centaurs, with its abundance of corpses both intended and incidental, shows
how shrewdly Eurystheus had calculated Hercules' task. Killing things came
easy to our hero – in fact he often accomplished it without trying. But he had
difficulty keeping even friends and family alive, let alone a homicidally-
inclined massive boar.

Capturing the Boar was a matter of balance. If Hercules tried to seize the
beast while it was still fresh, the maddened animal might kill him. However, if
the weakened beast succumbed to Hercules too late in the struggle it might
perish from the hero's ungentle attentions. Hercules needed to exercise his
judgement as much as his muscles for this task to be a success, and as the
episode with the centaurs demonstrates, sometimes the judgement of
Hercules was most notable by its absence. Hercules had evidently pondered
the matter, and decided that he could take advantage of the fact that driving
the centaurs to the brink of extinction had taken up much of the year. (By
some fanciful accounts the pursuit of the Boar itself also took a long time and
ended in the far corners of the known world. However the writers who claim
this, including the Roman philosopher Seneca and the fabulist Hyginus also
claim that Hercules killed the Boar, which would rather remove the point of
the exercise.)

Be that as it may, the point is that in Arcadia the mountains were now
covered in deep drifts of winter snow. This included Mt Erymanthos where we
can believe Hercules finally located his quarry. The immense strength of the
Boar was unequal to the even greater strength of Hercules, and in this case it
appears that Hercules was also the more cunning of the pair. He finished the
bout by executing a cunning plan. This involved stepping aside as the
exhausted and furious Boar launched a final wild charge.

Quite intentionally, Hercules was standing in front of a large snow-bank at
the time, and when he did his matador-style sidestep, the Boar whooshed by

71

and propelled itself deep into the snow - where it stuck fast. There is no mention of Athena in this Labour, possibly because the Goddess of Wisdom was been deeply offended by the unnecessary death of the learned Pholus and Cheiron. Therefore it seems that Hercules came up with the snowdrift idea himself, and so reduced his perilous task to a simple matter of digging out his prey before it perished from hypothermia.

Demonstrating a certain amount of pique, Hercules ignored the judges panel at the gates and with the Boar slung over his shoulder - where it had spent most of the past fortnight - he marched straight for the throne room of Eurystheus. Our hero's annoyance is understandable. He had neatly and all by himself captured a fearsome monster, yet all anyone could talk about was the collateral damage to Cheiron and Pholus. This remains the case even today – most discussion of the fourth Labour centres on centaurcide and treats the boar capture as almost incidental.

Hercules was aware of the blot on his legacy, and determined that the Boar should leave a lasting impression – and that impression should be made on the feet of Eurystheus when the Boar landed there. Even here Hercules was foiled. As we have seen, the under-rated Eurystheus had anticipated something of the sort. Our hero could do nothing but stand in frustration with the Boar wriggling in his arms while the voice of Eurystheus boomed in oracular fashion out of the buried bronze jar, congratulating Hercules (through gritted teeth) on the success of the current Labour. If Seneca and friends are correct that Hercules killed the Erymanthian Boar it may have been at this point, with the Labour completed and an outlet required for the hero's fury.

We do not know if it was on the same visit to the royal bronze jar that Hercules received his next assignment, but the nature of the task again shows how much midnight oil Eurystheus had burned in coming up with the idea. Our hero had proven himself unexpectedly diplomatic and cunning, as the Cerynitian Hind and the Erymanthian Boar had respectively demonstrated. That he was ferociously strong and courageous went without saying, though the Nemean Lion and Lernean Hydra might have added a comment or two.

So instead of something requiring strength, cunning, diplomacy or courage, perhaps Hercules might fail at an undignified task of mind-blowing tedium? Hercules could look the wildest monsters of mythology in the eye without blinking. But what about a pile of cattle droppings? A massive, monumental, pile of cow dung, which rather like the modern national debt, seemed to double in size every time one looked at it. For his next task, Hercules' mighty club and impenetrable lion-skin cloak would avail him naught.

A shovel might be handy though.

Elis is in the north west of the Peloponnese, a rugged area which has Arcadia to the east and Achaea to the north. At this time Elis was ruled by King Augeas, a man who was reputedly a child of Helios, the Sun God – the son of the Sun, one might say. Augeas was mighty and rich. In an era before money was commonplace, one way of measuring wealth was by cattle, and Augeas had more than a few of these.

Now had Helios turned his fiery steeds to the west, drawing the evening behind him. The fat flocks came from the pastures back to the farmyards and byres. Then came the cattle, thousands upon thousands.

Just as Notus, the south wind, or Boreas, the north wind drive the watery clouds before them across the heavens until the number of them above cannot be counted, and still there is no end to the new clouds that yet roll in to join those already there, until row climbs upon row and crest surmounts crest, in this way, in their cloud-like multitudes, those herds of cattle came still, up and on, on and up. Indeed, they filled the plain, and packed the paths upon it, the rich fields choked with moving cattle and their lowing. So were the stables made full of shambling cattle, and the sheep settled down for the night in the stockyards.

In truth, there were cows without number, and every man beside them worked frantically - here one hobbled their feet with cords cut straight and true so they might be led for the milking. Here another fed the thirsty yearlings with the warm, sweet milk of their mothers. This man again held the milking-pail, while another curdled the milk for good, fat cheese, and there another separated the bulls from the heifers.

Through it all King Augeas did his rounds of the stables to ensure his

herdsmen took good care of his property; and through all that great wealth which was his, his son [Phyleus] *came also.*
Theocritus, *Idylls* 25.5 ff

The problem was that with all these men doing all the milking and herding, Augeas seems to have neglected to assign anyone to the most basic of tasks - the shovelling clear of the nightly deposit of cow dung. As often happens with a task left for longer than it should be, eventually the sheer enormity of what had accumulated defeated even the intention to get started on it.

Even if Augeas reassigned his total manpower to the job there was no way that his men would make more than a dent in the problem - a dent that would be handily filled when the cows returned from the meadows the next day. Matters were reaching the point where Augeas would need either to raise the roofs in his stables, or relocate them altogether. The word *schadenfreude* would only be coined several millennia later, but the emotion of joy at another's misfortunes is probably as old as humanity. But while other kings saw only enjoyment at the problems of having too many cattle, King Eurystheus had seen an opportunity.

For his fifth Labour, Hercules had to clean the Augean stables. Not only would he have to shovel manure until the cows came home, when the cows came home his problems would really begin. After all, there were thousands and thousands of cows, and only one Hercules. Not to mention the substantial backlog.

Accordingly, Hercules took himself to Elis. Without mentioning the task with which he was charged, Hercules decided to study the lay of the land and arranged to stay with the king as a guest. He was after all, a prince of Thebes and one of the great heroes of Greece, which made him an ornament to any king's court. Theocritus tells us that Hercules accompanied the king and his son Phyleus on their evening rounds of the stables. (The king had other sons, but only Phyleus appears to have taken an interest in the family business.)

The next day Hercules and Phyleus wandered the meadows and the stretch of land between the rivers Peneios and Alpheios which flowed close by the stables. The Alpheios (the modern river Alfeios) was reputedly one of the longest rivers in the known world. After flowing 110km through the Peloponnese, as it still does, the mythological Alpheios plunged into an underground cavern and from there allegedly flowed through an underground lake to eventually emerge as the spring of Ortygia in Syracuse, Sicily. This was the same river later and memorably described by Samuel Taylor Coleridge as 'Alph, the sacred river ran /through caverns measureless to man/ down to a sunless sea.'

After a thoughtful contemplation of the local geography, Hercules came up with a plan that meant no-one would be building a pleasure-dome beside the river any time soon. That evening King Augeas completed his rounds. As he did so, Hercules pitched his offer.

Hercules would clean the royal stables, and furthermore, he would complete the task in one day, ensuring that the stables were pristine when the cattle returned to them in the evening. As a reward for this truly Herculean accomplishment, the hero asked for no more than a tenth of the king's cattle. Augeas may well have done a swift calculation. Doubtless Hercules was a handy fellow with a shovel, but it was equally beyond doubt that the hero had vastly under-estimated the task before him. He might well shift a substantial amount of the muck, but no-one could move all of that in a day. So there was no downside. Hercules would make at least a start on the long-delayed job, but failing in its accomplishment, he would leave unpaid. Therefore the king cheerfully agreed to the hero's terms.

The contract agreed, Hercules got to work. There was a lot to do, and he was working to a deadline. With Phyleus as a witness - though not as a helper, for Hercules had learned that much after the débâcle with the Lernean Hydra - the hero swiftly demolished part of the front wall of the stable.

Much of the evening was spent in the digging of mighty ditches between that breach in the stable wall and the rivers Peneios and Alpheios. Come dawn, when the cattle were led out to pasture, Hercules let the waters in. While the waters rushed and swirled about the stables, Hercules was at work around the back. At the right moment, he opened a breach in the back wall, and stood well back as a noisome flood of well-polluted water poured across the fields.

With Augeas' son Phyleus as his witness, Heracles made a breach in the foundations of the cattle-yard. He then diverted the courses of the Alpheios and

Peneios, which flowed near each other. He caused the rivers to flow into the stables, with an outlet for the water through an opening he had prepared earlier.
Apollodorus *Library* 2.5.5

We can certainly marvel at the ingenuity of Heracles. The task involved in this Labour was demeaning, yet he accomplished it without disgrace or doing anything to make himself unworthy of immortality.
Diodorus Siculus 4.13.3

How those living downstream from the Alpheios and Peneios rivers felt about this development is unknown. However, they could not have been more appalled than King Augeas who observed that his stables were sparkling clean and steaming off the damp into the afternoon air. However, the king had been doing some checking during the day.

At an acrimonious meeting that night he accused Hercules of concealing the fact that the cleaning of the stables was a Labour assigned by Eurystheus. Hercules doubtless responded that he also had not informed the Nemean Lion, the Hydra or any of the other subjects of his Labours about his intentions. Eventually it was decided that the matter should go to arbitration, and a bench of neutral judges was agreed upon. For the formal hearing Augeas had decided that on reflection his defence was rather weak, and he decided to settle for an outright lie instead. So the judges were asked to decide of Augeas had done a deal at all, rather than whether he should honour it. However, Hercules had a witness, and an honourable one at that.

The arbitrators had barely taken their seats when Phyleus was called by Heracles. He testified against his father and confirmed that a reward had been offered. Augeas flew into a rage and did not wait for the judges to vote. Both Phyleus and Heracles were ordered to get out of Elis.

Worse was to come - word got back to Mycenae of what had happened.

Eurystheus refused to count this Labour also among the ten, because [Hercules] had performed it as a hired man.
Apollodorus *Library* 2.5.5

We should observe that in ancient Greece the ideal was a nobleman who lived off the fruits of his estates. Far lower was the artisan who earned his living with his hands. Yet the gap between the nobleman and the artisan was at least as great as that between the artisan and the man who worked for hire. To the independent-minded Greeks an employee was a sort of voluntary slave. By saying that Hercules had been working for hire was an insult designed to rub salt into his already wounded pride - especially as the payment had not even been made. By now Hercules must have been lamenting that the Gods who had supplied his wondrous shield and helmet had lacked the foresight to also equip him with a really good lawyer.

Still, there were alternative courts of appeal. Hercules took up residence with Dexomenos, king of Olenos, who ruled a tidy little kingdom in Arcadia just over the border from Elis. There Hercules, the conqueror of Orchomenus, put out the word that he had a grudge against Augeas, king of Elis. Any enterprising young warriors with a taste for booty (or steak) were invited to join the cause. Hercules would return to Elis and Augeas would again be asked to honour his outstanding debt - and this time Hercules would not take 'no' for an answer.

His army was mainly Arcadian, but Apollodorus tells us that many of the foremost men of Greece sent squads of men. With every completed Labour, the legend of Hercules was growing. There were doubtless many who wanted to boast that they had fought alongside the mighty Hercules in war. While his men were gathering, Hercules passed the time outraging the hospitality of King Dexomenos by seducing his daughter. The affair came to light shortly before Hercules set off to war, but friendship with Dexomenos was preserved when Hercules promised to marry the lass on his triumphant return. However, things did not go to plan.

Augeas too had been mustering an army, and it was commanded by the stepsons of his brother Aktor, and these two were renowned; both as children of Poseidon and as the two best generals of the day. Hercules was outmanoeuvred in the field, and with his campaign at a critical point, the invincible hero fell sick. (Apollodorus, *Library* 2.7.2)

Already withdrawing, Hercules tried to buy time for his recovery by making a truce with the enemy. Once the reason for the truce became known, the sons of Aktor promptly resumed their attack and gave the Arcadian army a sound beating.

77

Meanwhile, back in Olenos, word of Hercules' engagement had come to the ears of a particularly vindictive exile. This was Eurytion, one of the centaurs who had fled the massacre at Mt Erymanthos and found safety in Arcadia. Now this mighty creature confronted King Dexomenos and demanded the hand of his daughter in marriage. The army of Dexomenos was off fighting with Hercules, and was no impressive body of men even when fully mustered. Dexomenos himself was no Hercules, and even one centaur was more than a match for most other Greek heroes. All the unfortunate king could do was put the date of the forced wedding as far in the future as possible and hope that his fortunes would change for the better.

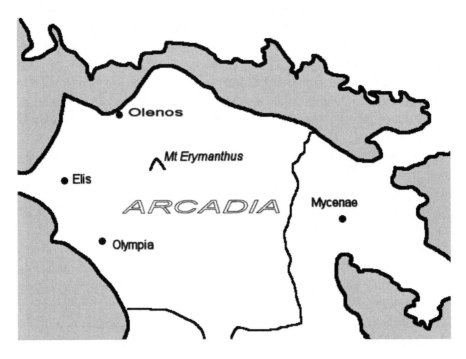

Hercules, on the other hand, was in the process of making his own fortune. Hearing that the enemy generals were off to give thanks and celebrate their victory at the third Isthmian festival to Apollo, the hero roused himself from his sick-bed. At a place called Kleonai he launched a decidedly un-heroic but very successful ambush that killed the brothers.

The morale of the remnants of the Arcadian army soared on the news that the mainstays of the enemy had perished. As arranged by Hercules beforehand, as soon as word arrived that the killing had been successful, the Arcadians set off for Elis at high speed. They arrived in Elis ahead of word of their coming, and easily smashed through the unprepared troops hastily gathered to oppose them. The war was ended at a stroke. The Eleans were leaderless, for Augeas now joined his generals in death, along with all his sons (apart from Phyleus). Phyleus was now restored to his homeland and his father's throne, and Hercules quickly agreed terms with the new regime.

To mark their achievement, Hercules and his army celebrated with a series of sporting events. A certain degree of vindictiveness creeps in even here, for Hercules took the chariot races instituted in memory of Pelops and expanded them into a full set of athletic events. In this way he subsumed a commemoration of the rival Pelopid family into the larger festival which he, a Perseid, now founded.

Also, Hercules chose to stage these games in Olympia at the sanctuary of Altis, the main feature of which was a temple to Hera – but he dedicated the games only to Zeus. At these games Hercules allegedly took part in and won every event, though Diodorus Siculus says this was because 'no-one was bold enough to contend with him'. The games continued to be celebrated thereafter, but the tradition of recording the winners of what became known as the Olympic Games only became established in 776 BC, so there exists no textual record of Hercules the *victor ludorum*.

Hercules had already claimed his cattle as the prize of war - and that was not all he claimed. In the text of Pseudo-Apollodorus we find listed a son of Hercules called 'Thestalos conceived on Epicaste, daughter of Augeas'. Hercules was a man of his time, and by modern standards he zig-zags from being heroic through grey areas into becoming an outright villain. Having conquered Elis, he almost certainly fathered Thestalos by rape, and doubtless considered himself fully entitled to do so.

His was a grimmer and far less scrupulous era, a time in which the offspring of an enemy were considered enemies themselves, no matter how innocent. Hercules had also been well aware that he was killing children when he slew his own offspring - however he had believed they were the children of Eurystheus and therefore fair game.

Nevertheless Hercules was also capable of coming to the aid of a lady in distress. His return to Olenos was timed to co-incide with the attempt of the centaur Eurytion to claim his bride. A short and fatal contest followed, so one-sided that mythologers have not bothered to record it. The name Eurytion means 'beautiful drinking vessel' and one might speculate both whether the appellation was given posthumously, and what part of the centaur was fashioned into the cup. In any case, two things became clear once Hercules had finished with Eurytion and pushed the centaur race further towards extinction.

Firstly, in having saved Dexomenos' daughter from a fate worse than death as a centaur's wife, Hercules had compensated for his earlier misconduct with the girl. His marriage to her was called off and the girl herself drops out of history, hopefully to have enjoyed a long and happy life with a husband less perilous than her two previous fiancées.

Secondly, despite fighting a brief but brutal war, making and breaking an engagement and cleaning out the Augean stables, Hercules had made no progress. With the current task disqualified, he was right back at Labour #3 where he had started.

Chapter 7

Of birds, bulls and Giants

The past year had seen the best and worst of Hercules. On the positive side, his destruction of the centaurs had proven that Hercules was indeed a force of nature comparable to a mid-range earthquake. With the Augean stables he had proven that his cunning was equal to his strength. His indomitable will was demonstrated by the unlikely come-back against the army of Elis. On the other hand .... .

The one-man war with the centaurs had driven that species to near-extinction taking with it notable creatures such as Pholus and Cheiron. And the *causus belli* was simply that neither Hercules nor the centaurs could keep their hands off a flagon of wine. At least the centaurs had the excuse of their own bestial natures. In wanting the wine opened in the first place, Hercules was self-indulgent and thoughtless at the very least, and his violent and unnecessary pursuit of the centaurs across Greece showed that he could be both vindictive and no less bestial than the creatures he hunted. In fact, for his conduct Hercules needed special dispensation from the Goddess Demeter 'that she might purify him of the guilt he had incurred in the slaughter of the Centaurs'. (Diodorus Siculus 4.14.13)

Furthermore, the entire Labour of the Augean stables would have been done and dusted in a week if Hercules had not lusted after the king's cattle, and made a fool of the king while winning them. (For in retrospect, what Hercules had done was obvious, and could have been achieved in a longer time by any king with an army to do the digging.) The result was a lost Labour and a needless war in which Hercules violated the rules of hospitality by seducing one girl and the rules of civilized conduct by raping another.

Finally, that war showed that Hercules could be beaten. The sons of Aktor had come close. Mighty Hercules had been forced to retreat and to ask for terms, and he had demonstrated his mortality by falling ill. So far Greece had seen only one Hercules - the unconquerable hero constrained only by the malice of Hera, and using even that to lay the flagstones on his road to glory. Now we get glimpses of another Hercules - the sly seducer and despoiler; petulant, vindictive and greedy, a man both vulnerable and prone to error and illness. So far these are but glimpses - yet as the story goes on, these glimpses eventually become the man, with but glimpses of the original Hercules showing through.

Given the duality of the nature of Hercules and the flaws which the past Labour had revealed, the question was which Hercules would come to the fore in the next Labour. Would the defects in the hero's character become greater and more obvious, or would Hercules return to his mid-season form? A lot depended on the nature of the Labour, and here again, Eurystheus demonstrated that his own ingenuity was far from exhausted. Hercules was off to Arcadia once more for his next round of monster-slaying, this time to the lake of Stymphalos.

There is a story they tell about the waters of Lake Stymphalos, that at one time man-eating birds bred on it. ... Among the many wild creatures found in the Arabian desert are those birds called Stymphalian, which are as much a menace to men as to lions or leopards. The birds fly against their hunters and wound or kill them with their beaks.

Men wearing bronze or iron armour are pierced by the birds, but Stymphalian birds can be caught in a garment woven from thick cork. For the beaks of the birds catch in the cork, just as the wings of small birds stick in bird-lime. These birds are of the size of a crane, but their beaks are more powerful, and not crooked like that of the ibis which they otherwise resemble.

Whether these modern Arabian birds are the same breed as the birds of old Arcadia, I do not know. But if there have always been Stymphalian birds, just as there have always been hawks and eagles, I would say these birds are of Arabian origin. Perhaps a flock of them once flew to Arcadia and reached Stymphalos. ... At Stymphalos there is also an old sanctuary of Stymphalian Artemis, the image being of wood, for the most part gilded. Near the roof of the temple have been carved, among other things, the Stymphalian birds. ... There are here also maidens of white marble, with the legs of birds, and they stand behind the temple.
Pausanias, *Guide to Greece* 8.22.4

This description by Pausanias was tailored for his more sceptical Roman audience, some of whom might even have been able to go to Arabia and check the birds there for themselves. The birds which Hercules was sent to clear from their lakeside retreat were altogether nastier than even a man-eating ibis with a super-powered beak. Perhaps this was because Ares, the God of War, had taken an interest in this particular flock. He had endowed them with feathers of bronze which the birds could shed in flight to fall like a rain of arrows on any hunter below. Furthermore - in something of an ongoing theme with the Herculean labours - the birds were poisonous. At least their dung was, and possibly their feathers as well.

The poisonous dung was a particular problem, for not only did the birds despoil the fruit trees of the region around the lake, but their dung polluted the soil and hindered the growth of fresh crops. (The orchards of Stymphalos still bear fruit today, particularly vine bushes which produce a grape which is dried and sold as 'Corinth Raisins'. Though the water level has dropped in recent millennia, Lake Stymphalos itself remains as it was those thousands of years ago – mostly a huge reed-filled marsh, too wet for ploughing and too solid for swimming.) From Eurystheus' point of view, this mission presented the chance that Hercules might fall victim to a shower of (possibly poisonous) bronze feathers, or die impaled upon a multitude of beaks. On the other hand, should the hero not fail and instead destroy the birds, he would incur the wrath of Ares whose special pets these birds were. In other words Eurystheus had tried to arrange things so that Hercules was damned if he did, and dead if he didn't. It was a pretty dilemma.

Fortunately our hero did not have to resolve it himself. Athena is notably absent from the story of Hercules in the previous two labours. Hercules was forced to capture the Erymanthian Boar by himself and attempt unaided his own disastrous form of diplomacy with King Augeas in Elis. The reason for this absence is quite probably that Athena was upset with her protégé for going above and beyond the call of duty in causing the deaths of Pholus and Cheiron. With their love of learning and teaching, these two could count themselves as servants of Athena, and both had perished as a direct result of Hercules' lack of self-control. So Athena had withdrawn her protection from the hero, something which also may explain his otherwise unaccountably

Athena, with all her trademarks; spear, helmet, aegis with Gorgon symbol, and owl
Sketch from a red-figure Etruscan Kylix c.470 BC now in the Vatican Museum

poor showing in the war with Elis. However, unlike Hera, Athena was not one to hold a grudge.

It will be recalled that Hercules' task was to clear the lake of the birds. Presumably Eurystheus hoped for the birds to be killed, and this would have made the task immensely more difficult, because the birds were said to 'cover the fields' with their numbers. However, Eurystheus was not so foolish as to incur the wrath of the God by directly instructing Hercules to slay a flock beloved by Ares. So he simply issued his demands in as general a fashion as possible and trusted to Hercules' natural talent for slaughter. This created a loophole in the job specification, and Athena intended Hercules to use it. The birds need not be killed if the lake could be rid of them in some other way.

Athena and the Craftsman God Hephaestus were close friends - as demonstrated by the fact that Hephaestus had remained alive after making an unsuccessful bid to force the Goddess' virginity. (The semen from this failed attempt fertilized the ground near Athens from which is said to have sprung the race of Athenians.) So Athena now prevailed on Hephaestus to construct a massive bronze cymbal - though 'cymbal' is only a rough translation of 'krotala', the Greek musical instrument which a cymbal most closely resembles. This krotala Hercules took to a 'mountain' near the lake. From the geography of the place, this can only have been the headland on the southern part of the lake where the town of Stymphalos was founded a generation or so later. (We know this because Homer tells us that men of Stymphalos fought in the Trojan War some fifty years afterwards.) Archaeology agrees with myth in this matter, having discovered enough Mycenaean settlement in the area for something like the birds to have been a nuisance, but no signs of the town of Stymphalos until later. Interestingly that later town's patron goddess appears to have been none other than Hera herself.

At the currently deserted headland Hercules whacked the cymbal against the side of the outcrop. The clang resounded across the lake, causing the panicked birds to rise in a body. The hero waited until the alarmed birds started to settle, and then clashed the cymbal again against the rocks. This caused the birds to take to the air once more. The process was repeated over and over, and Hercules being Hercules, he passed the time while waiting for the flock to settle back on the lake by shooting individual birds out of the air with his bow, thus adding to the consternation of the flock as a whole. Interestingly, there is a modern analogy for this technique of keeping birds airborne until exhausted. In 20th century China, as part of the 'four pests' campaign, the government pretty well managed to wipe out the Eurasian sparrow in Beijing by mobilizing the population to bang on pots and drums to keep the sparrows from settling down until the birds either fled or dropped from exhaustion. (Judith Rae Shapiro, *Mao's War Against Nature: Politics and the Environment in Revolutionary China.* Cambridge University Press, 2001)

In the same way, the Stymphalian Birds were unable to either settle back on the water or outlast Hercules. Finally they abandoned the lake and fled north-eastwards. The birds eventually settled down in the Euxine (Black Sea) area, appropriately enough on the Isle of Ares. There the feathered fiends were later encountered by Jason and his Argonauts.

With oars they clove the sea toward island of Ares, for at dusk the light breeze had fallen away. Then high above them, they spotted one of the birds of Ares which lived on that island. Hurtling toward them, it shook its wings down over the ship and sped on. A sharp-edged feather fell into the left shoulder of gallant Oileus, and he dropped his oar from his hands at the sudden wound ...

Then spoke Amphidamas, son of Aleus '...When Heracles came to Arcadia, not even he with his bow and arrow could drive away the birds that swam on the Stymphalian lake. I saw it myself. With a bronze cymbal in his hand he made a loud clashing sound as he stood upon a lofty peak, and the birds fled far off, screeching in bewildered fear.'
Apollonius *Argonautica* 1030-1050 *passim*

Taking their cue from Hercules, the Argonauts preserved themselves by banging their swords against their bronze shields causing the once bittern birds to shy away. Hercules himself would have been aboard to meet his old foes, but for an incident along the Argonauts' journey - a story to which we shall come in due course. However, we must return to the present, which sees Hercules making his way back to Eurystheus with a bird-free lake behind him. His current Labour had been completed in a brisk, business-like fashion and Eurystheus already had the next task lined up.

The Cretan Bull

This was a relatively straightforward Labour. Hercules had hit his stride, and

Eurystheus had not yet dreamed up some of the more outré tasks that were to make the later Labours so colourful. For the student of myth, this particular task is interesting because of the interplay of the saga of Hercules with the wider body of classical tales, especially the legend of Hercules' future friend and drinking buddy, Theseus.

While most people have never heard of the Cretan Bull, they are almost certainly familiar with his son, the Minotaur. The story of Theseus and the Minotaur belongs to another saga, but the opening parts of the tale are relevant here. They concern King Minos of Crete, the son of Zeus and that nymph Europa who gives modern Europe its name. In fact 'King Minos' is redundant, because in the Cretan language of the time 'minos' meant 'king'. But the Greeks who told the myths did not know that, and for them Minos was a person, and a person abundantly endowed with human flaws. One of these was greed. In return for a favour from Poseidon, Minos promised to sacrifice whatever the God sent him. The offer pleased Poseidon, who sent a magnificent snow-white bull. However, the Bull from the Sea was so splendid a beast that Minos could not bear to sacrifice the wondrous animal, and he substituted a lesser bull instead.

In his wrath, Poseidon cursed Pasiphae, the wife of Minos. As Hercules could testify, the vengeance of the Gods was sure and devastating, but the choice of victim was well short of discriminating. Any person in the line of fire, however innocent, counted as fair game. Under the influence of the curse, Pasiphae had the palace craftsman, Daedalus, construct for her a heifer of wood with a cowhide stretched realistically over the frame. Daedalus was unable to refuse the request because he had come to Crete as a refugee (he was wanted for murder in Athens) and was unwilling to give up his place of shelter. The statue he came up with was life-like but hollow, designed so that a woman divinely inflicted with lust might be able to wiggle into it. For this was the curse of Poseidon - that Pasiphae be filled with a monstrous passion for the Bull, and an urge to be mounted by it. And since even more than love, lust will find a way, the matter came to pass.

Now Pasiphae was herself no mere mortal, but a nymph of some power, for she was a daughter of Helios, the God of the Sun. Her sister was Circe, the island queen with a predilection for turning men into swine, and Pasiphae's niece was the termagant Medea, with her penchant for turning family members into corpses. Pasiphae had magical powers of her own, one of which kept Minos faithful through a spell that caused him to kill any concubine he attempted to sleep with. So it is perhaps unsurprising that Pasiphae not only managed to survive her union with the Bull but even to conceive a child.

This was the dread Minotaur, who may have looked cuter as a baby. However he still had the Bull's head and this was an immediate give-away to Minos that, though he was necessarily faithful, his wife had not been. Since no great powers of deduction were required to determine the father, the bull of Poseidon was driven from his comfy stall to fend for himself in the wild. This is the point at which the domestic troubles of Minos become entangled with the story of Hercules. The Bull became very successful at looking after itself, but did so at the expense of farmers and crops on the island. Furthermore it was now discovered that the creature possessed prodigious cunning which allowed it to evade whichever hunters the creature's great strength did not cause it to kill.

In short, the Bull was exactly the sort of creature that Hercules had become a specialist at disposing of. So King Minos sent a messenger to Eurystheus, and Eurystheus sent Hercules to Crete. The hero arrived, only to find that (by the account of Apollodorus) King Minos petulantly refused to give Hercules any help against the Bull which had once been his special gift from Poseidon. Eurystheus had forbidden Hercules to harm the Bull, possibly because he was uncertain how Poseidon felt about the matter. It was the Sea God's gift after all.

But above all, the stipulation that the creature had to be brought back to Mycenae alive was due to the diabolical cunning of Eurystheus. So large and savage was the Bull that no ship would carry the beast. So once Hercules had captured the Bull - a matter of routine - he had the interesting task of getting it from Crete to the mainland 'on his back across that wide expanse of sea' as Diodorus Siculus puts it. [4.13.4]

Two things make this task merely Herculean instead of downright impossible. The first was that the Bull was himself of an aquatic disposition, being the gift of Poseidon and from the sea in the first place. The second is that it is not a straight swim across the 500km between Crete and the mainland. Between the ports of Kissamos in western Crete and Neapoli on the Greek mainland lie the islands of Anticythera, Cythera and a string of small rocky islets. So if Hercules followed the route of the modern ferry, but landed on each small

Engraving by Bernard Picart from 1731 of Hercules crushing the Cretan Bull

islet instead of conscientiously avoiding it, he could have done the trip with a maximum of about 25 kilometres between stops. Certainly this would have required a degree of navigational knowledge, but not even the supernatural intervention of Athena would have been needed for this. The route was well-known to the island-hopping Greek sailors of the day. One can imagine the deep blue of the Aegean Sea on a cloudless morning, and the crew of a *syros*-type Minoan trader gaping from the ship's rail at the sight of Hercules doing a lazy side-stroke through the translucent water, towing by one horn the complaining Bull that thrashed along beside him.

The Bull was duly presented to Eurystheus and then, Hercules having no further interest in the beast, and no-one being certain whether Poseidon agreed to it being killed, the Bull was simply left to its own devices. It eventually finished up on the plain of Marathon outside Athens, and there became the same sort of public menace that it had been in Crete. Eventually it was killed by Theseus. (Poseidon was the father of Theseus, which allowed that hero to take certain liberties with the God's creatures.)

Thus Hercules had completed yet another Labour in a workmanlike manner with no margin for Eurystheusan quibbles. In fact Hercules was hereafter to ensure that he left no grounds for Eurystheus to challenge the successful completion of a Labour, so when the two disqualified Labours are added to the remainder that the hero was obliged to complete, the number comes very satisfactorily to the sacred number of twelve. As a further footnote to this seventh (or fifth) Labour, Hercules evidently made a deep impression on the Cretans during his brief stay. Even today the main town of the island is Heraklion (pop. 174,000).

The War with the Giants

Diodorus Siculus, whose chronology of the deeds of Hercules is the most consistent of the various authors who tell the story, places at this point a huge disturbance in the heavenly order of things - an upheaval which, by compa-rison, made the labours of Hercules seem both trivial and mundane.

In a way Hercules himself was the catalyst who brought about a challenge to the Olympian Gods and the order on Earth which the Gods were slowly establishing. The extent of the danger cannot be over-stated. Zeus was God of Order, and to some extent the order of things on Earth was his order. Until the

Olympian Gods had come into their power, the Earth had been a chaotic place in which the average unfortunate mortal could not even be sure of what shape he would awaken in the morning. It was the Olympians who set the frame upon the world, and established certain basic principles, such that today would be followed by tomorrow. (This late organization of Time might explain some of the chronological aberrations in the Hercules legend). In fact, in his Labours Hercules was acting as a sort of odd-job man on an epic scale, clearing up elements such as the children of Typhon which lingered on from the chaotic early days of the world. Now it looked as though the entire apple-cart of the cosmos was about to be overturned and the bad old days would come roaring back.

The problem was the Giants. These days 'giants' refers to creatures of extraordinary size, but the meaning is actually 'earth-born'. The 'earth' in question is mother Gaia, and the Earth-born were 'gaia gentes' or 'gigantes'. Their size was far from trivial: 'They were unequalled in the bulk of their bodies and invincible in their power; terrible in appearance, with long hair sweeping from head and chin, and dragon-scale on their feet,' says Apollodorus in *Library* 1.6.2. (Just as Diodorus gives us the best chronology of the event, Apollodorus gives us the most detail, so his account will be followed here, with other sources intervening as appropriate.)

The Giants were children of Uranus, Zeus' grand-daddy. Uranus knew that he would be deposed by his son, so as each child was born of Gaia, he stuffed it back into its mother. Gaia held these children within herself, but when upset with Zeus (who had been unkind to some of her other children) she released the Giants into the world.

For an uncounted time there was an uneasy truce between Olympians and Giants. While still unmarried, Hera had a dalliance with a Giant.

They say that when Hera was still a maid, she fell in love with Eurymedon, one of the Gigantes, and by him bore the child Prometheus. Zeus knew of this, and consequently threw Eurymedon into Tartarus, and when Prometheus stole fire from the Gods, Zeus used this excuse to chain him to the rock.
(Schol. T. ad II 14.296)

Things were not exactly amicable. When in the region of Olympus the Giants were in the habit of taking rocks 'heavier than a strong man could lift' and lobbing them at the Gods on the summit. As an alternative form of vandalism they would ignite trees and throw the burning trunks at Olympus like fiery spears. A reading of Pindar's Isthmian Ode suggests that Alcyoneus, one of the leaders of the Giants - they numbered over a hundred - brought things to the brink of war by stealing the cattle of Helios, God of the Sun. But what tipped things over the edge was Hercules.

It was ordained by Fate that the Gods could not kill the Giants unless a mortal man helped in the slaying. Until Hercules came along the Giants were reasonably confident that before a fight got properly started they could crush any participating mortal like a bug. Hercules was a different matter, as the prophet Tiresias had pointed out at Hercules' birth.

He said that when the Gods meet the Giants in battle on the plain of Phlegra, the shining hair of the Giants will be stained with dirt as they fall beneath the rushing arrows of that hero.
Pindar *Nemean Odes* 1

That put a different complexion on things.

Learning of this, Gaia created a potent herb which would prevent the Giants from being destroyed even by a mortal. But Zeus banned the dawn and ordered the moon and the sun not to shine. Then in darkness he harvested all of the herb himself before anyone else could get at it.
Apollodorus *Library* 1.6.2

Zeus sent Athena to pick up Hercules with orders to prepare for war. Matters had come to the crunch and Zeus needed Hercules in his prime for the coming struggle, which would be soon, as Zeus needed to crush the Giants before Gaia was more successful with her next herbal concoction.

Nor were the Giants unwilling to meet the Gods in battle. As children of Uranus they were the elders, and felt that Zeus and his fellow Gods of the next generation had pre-empted their right to rule on Earth. By some accounts the Giants opened the hostilities by a march on Olympus, but this is an obvious conflation with the much earlier War of the Titans, which is the war by which Zeus and his fellow Gods came to power in the first place.

In fact it appears that Gods took the initiative, and brought the war to the

Giants. The struggle was resolved in at least two major battles. The first of these was at Pallene, the modern Kassandra Peninsula which is the most westerly of the three finger-like peninsulas reaching into the Aegean sea south of Thessalonika. This was the birthplace of Alcyoneus, the solar cattle-rustler and one of the leaders of the Giants. In the course of the struggle Alcyoneus and Hercules met in personal combat. This duel put to the test the idea that the Giants could only be killed with the intervention of a mortal man.

We should note that Zeus was all the readier to risk Hercules in this death match because he had the God Dionysus in reserve. Like Hercules, the androgynous God of Wine was fathered by Zeus off a mortal woman and might possibly be construed as human through a good legalistic argument. For all his girlish appearance, this war proved Dionysus to be a remarkably mean fighter who brained at least one of the leading Giants with his Thyrsus (staff).

However, the back-up demi-god was not required because Hercules handily dealt with Alcyoneus on his own. There was one worrying development - though Hercules shot the Giant dead with a well-placed arrow, Alcyoneus somehow struggled back to life. Was Hercules insufficiently mortal to meet the terms of the prophesy? Athena stepped in with the solution.

Alcyoneus was immortal so long as he fought in the land of his birth. ... Heracles first shot him with an arrow, so when the Giant fell to the ground he somehow revived. Therefore, at Athena's advice Heracles dragged him outside Pallene, and once off his native soil the Giant died.
Apollodorus *ibid*

From here the war moved to the Campi Flegrei near Naples. The argument that Pallene was also called Phlegra should be disregarded. Phlegra means 'burning' and the 'burning fields' near Naples and Cumae (both Greek colonies) fit the description perfectly, while nothing on the Pallene peninsula comes close. Even today the smoking, cratered landscape near Vesuvius looks like the aftermath of exactly the sort of battle the Greeks imagine the Gods fought against the Giants. A large chunk of the 'burning fields' now bubble away under water in the Gulf of Pozzuoli. This is because when the Giant Enceladus tried to flee southward, Athena ripped up that chunk of land and whacked him with it, either creating or substantially adding to that part of the island of Sicily which now has Enceladus embedded in the foundations. Thereafter, discovering that the Giant Pallas had an unbreakable skin, Athena imitated Hercules with the Nemean Lion. She killed and skinned her enemy on the battlefield and the invulnerable shield thus created, the Aegis, has passed from myth into general use in the English language.

Elsewhere the Battle of Phlegra forced teamwork from some unlikely partners. Hercules found himself back-to-back with his step-mother Hera in a losing fight with another of the enemy champions, a monster called Porphyrion, whom the poet Pindar calls 'the king of the Giants'. The pair were losing the struggle when Zeus stepped in to afflict Porphyrion with an overwhelming lust for Hera. Porphyrion promptly stopped trying to take Hera's life and concentrated on taking her virtue instead. It is indicative of the relationship between Zeus and Hera that Zeus chose that form of distraction in order to see how much Hera resisted the sudden development. As soon as Hera called for help, the would-be battlefield rapist was hit by a one-two combination of a thunderbolt from Zeus and an arrow in the eye from Hercules. As prophesied, the joint strike by mortal and god proved lethal.

From here, Hercules moved across the field as the finisher to each divine victory. When Apollo shot a Giant in the left eye, Hercules put another into the right. As we have seen, Dionysus got his kill, dread Hecate got another, and Poseidon, disdaining the help of Hercules, followed the example of Athena and, after chasing his victim across the Mediterranean, dropped an island (modern Nisyros) on him. The Fates, Hephaestus and the others made their contribution, but most of the slaughter was accomplished by the team of Zeus and Son.

The other Giants Zeus smote and destroyed with thunderbolts and all of them Heracles shot with arrows as they were dying.
Apollodorus *ibid*

The aftermath of the battle is described by Diodorus Siculus as follows

When the Giants of Pallene decided to make war against the immortal Gods, Heracles fought alongside the Gods. He received the highest praise for the manner in which he slew so many of the Sons of Earth. Thereafter Zeus gave the name of 'Olympian' only to those Gods who had fought by his side ...

Of those born of mortal women only Dionysus and Heracles were thought worthy of this name, not only because they had Zeus for their father, but because they were of a like mind to him and worked for the betterment of humanity.
Diodorus Siculus *History* 4.15.1

Hercules had played an essential part in this gigantic struggle. It turned out that the Gods, though far fewer, were more than a match for the Giants. But had Hercules not been around to finish off each bout, the Giants might have held on indefinitely. As it was, the Giants joined the centaurs on the list of species which Hercules had helped drive towards extinction. Of course some Giants still live today, for Hercules was unable to finish off those upon whom the Gods had dropped significant pieces of geography. These survivors still fume beneath the Earth, periodically venting their wrath in spectacular volcanic eruptions.

Chapter 8

Hercules goes north – horses and fleeces

With the return of Hercules from the wars, the job of Eurystheus had become that much harder. Hercules had done well in the battles with the Giants, and now more than ever enjoyed the favour of Zeus. Perhaps - for a short while - even Hera felt slightly less bitter about Hercules now that the pair had been comrades-in-arms. Therefore we note a change in emphasis in the remaining Labours – a change possibly inspired by the time it took for Hercules to return with the Cretan Bull. The Labours become less about contriving for Hercules to come to a messy death, because Eurystheus had by now decided that Zeus was unlikely to forgive him for that. Instead Hercules is sent as far from Mycenae as possible, on the basis that travel in the world of myth was a dangerous business, and Eurystheus could hardly be blamed for an incidental death on the road. Furthermore, the more distant the Labour, the longer it kept Hercules away from Mycenae, and that was just fine with Eurystheus. He was running out of local monsters anyway.

Therefore during his midnight contemplation, the king would have sorted through the various possibilities, and given a high raking to King Diomedes of Thrace. Thrace was more or less the Wild East of mythology - a place even less organized than the rest of the still untidy cosmos. It was the home of witches, exotic monsters and highly uncivilized humans. Specimen One of the latter group was King Diomedes himself. The name 'Diomedes' means 'thought of Zeus', though Zeus must have thought that name highly inappropriate. Among the various aspects in his portfolio, Zeus was God of Hospitality – yet Diomedes did not entertain his guests but instead, as he did with all strangers to his realm, he fed them to his horses.

...their manes are uncurried, their hair falls shaggy down to their hoofs, and

96

*they are like wild beasts in every way. Their stalls reek from the flesh and bones
of the men whom Diomedes has used as food for these horses, and the keeper of
the mares is himself even more savage in his conduct than the horses.*
Philostratus, *Imagines* 2.25

There were four of these mares. The *Fabulae* (30,9) of Hyginus list them as
follows: Podargos the fleet-footed, Lampon the shining one, Xanthos the
saffron, and Deinos the terrible - creatures of massive strength made
ferociously savage by their unnatural diet 'with unbridled jaws they greedily
champ their bloody food at gore-splattered mangers, devouring human flesh
with ghastly delight', says the playwright Euripides (*Madness of Heracles* 380).
The mission of Hercules - and he had no choice but to accept it - was to bring
these beauties back alive to Eurystheus.

Because it was assumed that King Diomedes and perhaps also his people -
the Bistones - would object to a stranger turning up and unceremoniously
removing the horses, Hercules was allowed to take volunteers to assist in this
Labour. There was no shortage of such volunteers, for many now wished to
claim that they had been at the side of mighty Hercules as he performed his
already-famous Labours. To his lasting regret, Hercules agreed to the pleading
of a young favourite of his and allowed a son of the God Hermes, a youth
called Abderus, to come along on this adventure.

Some of the later peripatetic labours describe in detail the journey of
Hercules to the site of the actual deed, and carefully list the extra-curricular
corpses which he piled up along the way. Yet in this case there are almost
details whatsoever of how the hero and his band of adventurers got to Thrace,
possibly because they did not want Diomedes to know they were coming.
After all, news like Hercules tended to spread fast, so the team would have
wanted to move swiftly and inconspicuously to stay ahead of rumour. As a
result we know from a single verb in Apollodorus that the adventurers 'sailed'
to Thrace, but nothing else of the journey, apart from one remarkable
incident. In fact, so remarkable was this incident that a brief digression is
called for.

We have met Jason and his Argonauts on their way to retrieve the golden
Fleece. The man who sent Jason on his mission was King Pelias. Now this king
comes into our story again, as the father of the fair Alcestis. Alcestis was
married to Admetus. The pair were deeply in love, but in his hurry to

consummate his marriage, Admetus forgot to sacrifice to Artemis. The vengeful Goddess filled Admetus' bed with venomous snakes, and for a while it seemed Alcestis would be a widow before she was properly a wife.

The nightmares
Detail from a painting by Luca Giordiano (1632-1705)

However, Apollo had a soft spot for the couple, and indeed had played Cupid in their romance. Consequently Apollo persuaded the Fates that the life of Admetus would be spared if someone agreed to die in his place. Oddly enough, no-one could be found to take up this generous offer, not even the aged parents of Admetus. In the end Alcestis decided to sacrifice herself for her husband's life. Death to the Greeks was Thanatos, the child of Night and the brother of Sleep. When pale Thanatos came for Alcestis, he found Apollo waiting with a warning.

According to Euripides, Apollo informed Thanatos:

Savage and brutal as you are, you shall be stopped. Even now, he who will stop you travels to this house, despatched by Eurystheus to steal a team of horses from wintry Thrace. He shall be a guest here in Admetus' house. Then shall he steal the woman away from you by force. You will not have our gratitude [for voluntarily leaving Alcestis alive], *and indeed you will have my hate, but you shall still not have the woman.*
Euripides *Alcestis* 45ff

Sure enough Hercules arrived and was informed of events. He laid out his plan.

I must save this woman who has so recently died. I will bring Alcestis back to dwell again in this house, and in this way repay the kindness of Admetus. I shall go [to the tomb] *and keep watch for Thanatos in his robe of shadow. This master of the dead I believe I shall find drinking the blood of the beasts sacrificed beside the grave. I shall ambush him from hiding. When caught I shall crush him with my encircling arms. Nor shall he escape my hold on his bruised ribs, until he surrenders the woman to me.*
Euripides *Alcestis* 839ff

The story as told by Euripides ends with things going exactly as planned. Thanatos is beaten up, and Hercules and restores Alcestis to her husband. Then, like a good hero, Hercules rides off into the sunset, declaiming 'Farewell! I go now to perform the labour assigned to me by the tyrant son of Sthenelus'.

The next time we hear of Hercules, he and his men have completed their journey to Thrace and are already at the stables, having driven off the guards.

At this point an unexpected difficulty arose, because the horses were so savage that they were actually held close to their blood-splattered brass mangers by thick, solid chains. One can assume that Hercules had worked out the time required for taking the horses and fleeing before Diomedes and his men could catch him, but breaking these chains slowed things down. Furthermore, Hercules had necessarily to work on the principle that Diomedes would delay long enough to gather enough men for his purpose. When one's purpose is defeating Hercules, that means assembling a small-to-medium-sized army. However, Diomedes appears to have assumed that the reputation of Hercules was over-blown, for he set off in pursuit with a hastily-gathered force built more for speed than strength.

Consequently, while Hercules succeeded in driving the mares to the coast, he got no further before he had to muster his men to fight off Diomedes in a rearguard action. Abderus was too young and unskilled for combat, so Hercules left his young favourite in charge of the mares while he and the rest of his men set off to do battle. This battle was a short, sharp affair in which the last thing Diomedes ever knew was that Hercules was every bit as lethal as his reputation claimed him to be. 'Heracles fought against the Bistones, slew Diomedes and compelled the rest to flee.' [Apollodorus *Library* 2.5.8]

Triumph turned to tragedy when the adventurers returned to their camp, and there beheld a scene both horrific and tragic. Evidently the mares had attempted to bolt. Young Abderus, doing his duty to the last, had hung on grimly to the traces and been dragged to death. Distracted by the scent of blood, the horses had then stopped their flight and settled down to feed. The creatures had barely managed to sink their teeth into their ghastly meal when Hercules came upon them. The subsequent scene was captured in a painting, ancient even in classical times, when it was described thus:

The Mares of Diomedes were no challenge for Heracles, since [in the picture] *he has already overcome them and crushed them with his club. One mare lies on the ground, another is gasping for breath, a third appears to be reeling away while the fourth collapses, stunned ...*

Heracles has snatched from the mares the half-eaten body of Abderos. Going by the pieces, still beautiful, which remain it appears that the horses devoured a tender youth. Heracles carries these remains on his lionskin. [We can imagine] *the tears he shed over them, the embraces he may have given them, the laments he cried, the grief heavy on his features.*
Philostratus, *Imagines* 2.25

Hercules decided to give the mares one last meal of human flesh. The body of Diomedes was dishonoured as Diomedes had desecrated many a corpse before – by being fed to his horses. Sated by the corpse of their former owner, the mares became amenable. In fact, so much so that Hercules decided to hitch them to a quadriga - a four horse chariot - and properly tame the beasts. 'He mounted on a chariot and tamed with the bit the horses of Diomedes', says Euripides (*ibid*)

Abderus was given a magnificent funeral, and as a lasting memorial to the youth, Hercules founded the city of Abdera beside the tomb. Some of the adventurers who had accompanied Hercules on his mission north may have been the first settlers - after all Thrace was rich, and they now had the kingdom of the late Diomedes at their disposal. The city later gave birth to the lyric poet Anacreon, but was in decline even in the 4th century BC. Every year that the city existed, the memory of Abderus was celebrated with games. The events included wresting, running and boxing - but not chariot racing or anything else horse-related. That would have been insensitive.

Having tamed the infamous horses of Diomedes to the bit, one can imagine that Hercules took the opportunity to promote his legend by driving his chariot south through Thrace, Thessaly and on to the Peloponnese, gathering crowds at every stop. Eventually arriving in Mycenae, Hercules handed the horses to Eurystheus. In one of his less tactful moments, Eurystheus dedicated the man-eating beasts to Hera and then released them. 'Eventually they came to Mt Olympus, as they say, and there were killed by wild wild animals', concludes Apollodorus. But at least one of the horses may have survived; for Diodorus Siculus insists that the breed 'continued to the reign of Alexander of Macedon' [*History* 4.15.4]. This has led to speculation that 'ox-headed' Bucephalus, the gigantic black horse of Alexander the Great, was a descendant of those beasts captured and tamed by Hercules.

Hercules and the Argonauts

At this point we run into again into a problem of chronology, though the matter is a minor one. A new narrator picks up the tale, Apollonius of Rhodes, who wrote in the third century BC, which was about a thousand years after the events he describes. Given this lapse in time, a certain degree of inexactitude is excusable - especially as Hercules is an incidental character in the saga which Apollonius is telling. This is the story of Jason and his Argonauts and their journey to the fabled land of Colchis to obtain the legendary Golden Fleece.

How the Fleece got to Colchis in the first place need not concern us here. That Jason had to retrieve the thing is more relevant, because the intent of the king who sent Jason was exactly similar to the intent of Eurystheus for Hercules. That is, the king (rightly) saw Jason as a threat to himself, and so sent him on a mission that he hoped would kill him but which would in any case keep Jason away from his kingdom for as long as possible. What follows is extracted from the *Argonautica*, the tale told by Apollonius, with commentary added as appropriate. We begin as Jason is gathering all the greatest heroes of Hellas to join his crew. (All the texts quoted in the following passages are extracts from various parts of the *Argonautica* of Apollonius.)

Jason; leader of the fearless Argonauts
From a red-figure vase c.465 BC now in the Metropolitan Museum of Art, New York

We discover that great-hearted Heracles did not disregard the eager summons of Aeson's son [i.e. Jason]. *He was on the road carrying alive the boar that fed in the thickets of Lampeia, near the vast Erymanthian swamp when rumours of the muster of the heroes reached him … At the entrance of the market place of Mycenae he set down from his mighty shoulders the boar bound with chains.*

Then of his own volition and against the wish of Eurystheus he set off; and

with him came his brave comrade Hylas, in the prime of his youth, to bear the
quiver of Heracles and to guard his bow.
Apollonius *Argonautica* 1.122

This is where our chronological problem comes in, because it is clear that Apollonius sees Hercules as getting the news even as he captured the Erymanthian Boar, and thereafter setting off to join the Argonauts as soon as practically possible. This simply does not work, as we know that after Hercules captured the Boar he actually fought two wars - one against Augeas and the other with the Giants - and wrapped up another four Labours before joining Jason's crew. This is not indicative of frantic haste. Therefore we may assume that Apollonius has confused the capture of the man-killing Erymanthian Boar with the capture of the man-eating horses of Diomedes. Once we make this assumption, and have Hercules hearing of the muster of the heroes as he drove his chariot south through Greece, the adventure with Jason and his Argonauts dove-tails neatly into the saga of Hercules.

Without Hylas, we would never have heard of Theiodamas and an example of Herculean thuggery which may have been more common than the legend lets on. Theiodamas was ploughing his land when he was approached by Hercules, who demanded his ox, presumably for a meal. 'Hercules desired him to give up the ox against his will', the poet tells us, and when Theiodamas refused, the hero 'pitilessly slew him'. This escalated into a war between Hercules and Theiodamas' people; a war which ended with Theiodamas' tribe being driven from their land and young Hylas, the son of Theiodamas, taken by Hercules as the spoils of war. Some later writers justify this by claiming that Theiodamas' people were illegally squatting on their land, and Hercules was looking for a pretext to start the fighting. But when we look at Hercules' later record, straightforward murder and robbery are just as likely. Hellas in those days was a rough place, where 'the strong did what they could, and the weak suffered what they must,' (as the historian Thucydides later put it), so the deed did no harm to the hero's reputation.

In fact Hercules was by far the most prestigious of the Argonauts, so on his arrival there was a popular movement to make him the leader of the expedition.

With the heroic Heracles in their number, the young heroes turned their gaze upon him. With one voice they loudly urged him to take up the leadership. But he, from the place where he sat, stretched out his right hand saying, 'Do not offer me this honour. I will not agree to take it, and I will not allow anyone else to put himself forward. The hero who brought us together here should be the leader of our company.'

When these noble sentiments had been uttered, they agreed to do as Heracles said, so warlike Jason stood with a glad heart ...
ibid 1.341

In a modern rowing eight, the middle seats are referred to as 'the engine room'. This was also true of the *Argo*, for Hercules took the middle - indeed he could hardly have done otherwise 'for the keel sank deep beneath him'. The *Argo* was built of sacred wood, so that the ship could speak for itself. Other versions of the saga of the Argonauts have the ship complaining bitterly about the weight of Hercules, or indeed, refusing to carry him altogether.

The opening stages of the voyage to Colchis took the *Argo* to the isle of Lemnos. And there the voyage might have ended. The womenfolk of Lemnos had lost (or says Apollonius, had murdered) their menfolk, and by the time the Argonauts turned up they were desperate for male company. This the Argonauts happily supplied.

Straight away the city rejoiced with dances and banquets ... with songs and sacrifices to the illustrious son of Hera and Cypris [Aphrodite] herself. And sailing off was constantly postponed from one day to another. They might have lingered there indefinitely, had not Heracles gathered his comrades apart from the women, and reproachfully addressed them

'You wretches ... do we so despise the women of our native land that we have come here to get married? Is it now the plan to live here and plough the rich soil of Lemnos? We do our reputations no good dallying here with a crowd of female strangers. Or did you think that some god is going to grant a prayer so that the Fleece will come to us all by itself? ....'

After this lecture, no-one dared to meet his eye, or say a word in their defence. Instead while they were all gathered, they prepared to depart in haste.
ibid 1.842-1865 passim

And so onward, toward the kingdom of Cyzicus between the Aegean and the Black Sea on the Sea of Mamara which the ancients called the Propontis.

There is an island in the Propontis ... which those living thereabouts call the Mount of Bears. Savage, fierce men dwell there whom they call the 'Earth-born'. These are wondrous to their neighbours because each one can raise six mighty hands, two from his sturdy shoulders, and four tight-fitted to his fearsome sides below. These Earth-born rushed down from the mountain ... but there Heracles remained with the younger heroes. Quickly he bent his back-springing bow and brought the monsters one after another to the ground. In response they picked up huge jagged rocks and hurled them. For it is my opinion that these awful monsters, like the others, had been raised by the goddess Hera, bride of Zeus, to be a trial for Heracles.
ibid 1.936-1.989 passim

The monsters were driven off or slain, and a number of friends died too. For the winds drove the Argonauts back by night to what they supposed was the same island. In fact it was a neighbouring island, whose normally hospitable inhabitants assumed that the night-time visitors were raiders. By the time it had been established that the Argonauts were not pirates and the islanders were not Earth-born, Hercules had already finished off two of the leading heroes on the opposing side. Thereafter the winds died off altogether, though this was not a problem.

The mighty arms of Heracles carried the weary rowers along, and made even the well-built timbers of the ship shiver. Her bow ploughed a furrow through the rough waters, but he was too eager to reach the mainland ... and snapped his oar in the middle. He fell sideways, one half of the oar held in both hands, the other swept away in the ship's wake. In silence Heracles sat up, glaring around.
ibid 1.1155

At that point it would probably have been fatal for anyone to so much as crack a smile at Hercules' pratfall so, straight-faced, the Argonauts picked up their oars and pulled for the nearest island. There Hercules intended to uproot a suitably sturdy tree and make an oar of it while his comrades made their dinner. Apollonius relates what happened next:

The son of Zeus told his comrades to enjoy their meal while he headed for the woods to make an oar suitable for his hands. After some exploration, he found a thick, strong pine, tall and straight as a poplar and without too many leaves or branches. He swiftly set his arrow-laden quiver and bow on the ground, and stripped off his lion-skin cloak.

After loosening the roots of the pine with his bronze-tipped club, he wrapped his hands around the bottom of the trunk. With his legs braced, he pressed it to his broad shoulder and by strength alone pulled the deep-rooted tree from the ground with clumps of earth still clinging to it. When at the stormy setting of ill-omened Orion a swift blast of wind comes unexpectedly from the sky and the ship's mast - wedges and all - is pulled from its tether; so did Heracles uproot the pine. Then he picked up his bow and arrows, his lion-skin and club, and made his way back.

Meanwhile Hylas also had left the group to go with a bronze pitcher in hand to seek the sacred waters of a fountain. He wanted to swiftly draw water and get everything ready for his master's return. ... He quickly came to the spring which the locals called Pegae.

Now it happened that all the nymphs who dwelt in that lovely headland were in the habit of praising Artemis every night in song and their dance for that night was beginning. The nymphs of the peaks and the glades were already ranging far into the woods, but the water-nymph was just rising from the sweet-flowing spring. She saw the lad nearby, and the full moon in the sky showed him in the bloom of his beauty and sweet charm. Cypris [Aphrodite] made her heart so weak that in her confusion she almost lost her wits. But he leaned sideways and dipped his pitcher into the water which rang loud as it fell into the echoing bronze. At once she put her left arm over his neck, and with her right she pulled down his elbow, and yearning to kiss his tender mouth, she plunged him into the rippling water.

The hero Polyphemus, son of Eilatus was the only one to hear the boy cry out, for he had gone up the path to meet Heracles on his return. He dashed toward Pegae in the direction of the cry, like a forest predator who has heard sheep bleating has from afar ... fearing that the lad had been taken by wild beasts he quickly drew his great sword, fearing also that someone had ambushed him travelling alone and carried him off as easy prey. Thus, brandishing a naked sword in his hand, he ran into Heracles himself on the path ... and straight away he told of the wretched calamity with labouring heart and panting breath.

When Heracles heard his words, sweat poured in torrents from his temples and the black blood boiled beneath his heart. In his fury he hurled the pine to the ground and rushed recklessly down the path, hardly heeding where he put his feet. Like a bull maddened by a gadfly he tore along, unchecked ... in his frenzy he pumped his knees without rest, but now again paused in his effort and shouted far with a loud pealing cry.
ibid 1187ff

All night Hercules searched, and by day he was far from the camp-site. The Argonauts had no idea of where Hercules had gone, only that he had mysteriously left them. The wind had sprung up, and after waiting as long as they could, the Argonauts decided to press on with their quest. Even then a conscience-stricken Jason would have turned back but the 'sons of Thracian Boreas' stopped him. While the heroes were debating what to do:

There appeared from the depths of the sea, Glaucus, the wise interpreter of [the sea god] *Nereus. Raising high his shaggy head and chest he seized the ship's keel with his sturdy hand calling to the eager crew.*

'Do you propose to take bold Heracles [on this quest] *against the wish of mighty Zeus? He is fated to complete all his twelve labours for insolent Eurystheus before he goes to live among the immortals. He has a fair few to complete yet, so feel no regret for leaving him. ... out of love a goddess-nymph has made Hylas her husband.'*
ibid 1.1301

Hylas and the Nymphs
Detail from a painting by John Waterhouse (1896) now in the Manchester Art Gallery

So the heroes sailed on to complete their quest, much to the relief of the poet. For had Hercules stayed, the subsequent challenges would have been much less, and the excitement of the tale greatly diminished. The other heroes would have simply stood back and let Hercules do the heavy lifting. In time the *Argonautica* would have been entitled 'How Hercules won the Golden Fleece', and Jason would have dropped into obscurity.

It was better all round that Hercules be left marooned, and Jason should meet Medea, and carry the Fleece home in unshared triumph. Naturally Hercules did not see things quite that way, and years later he made a special effort to find those sons of Thracian Boreas who had refused to turn back to get him. 'When they were returning from the games he slew them in sea-girdled Tenos and heaped the earth over them.'

For now, currently stranded on the island, Hercules and Polyphemus set about fulfilling their different destinies. Polyphemus founded a great city at the mouth of the river, while Hercules found passage to the mainland, threatening to return and devastate the place if the islanders did not bring him news of what had become of Hylas, be he living or dead.

The Argonauts did later find what had become of Hercules, as they later met someone who had met him on his further adventures.

Friends, that was some man from whose help you have fallen away ... here he entered in the ring to box with Titias, mighty Titias who surpassed all the other young men in strength and beauty. Him Heracles killed and tumbled all his teeth to the ground.

Allied with the Mysians he subdued the Phrygians who inhabit the lands beside ours and brought them under my father's rule. He made his own the land and tribes of Bithynia from the mouth of [the river] *Rhebas and the peak of Colone. The Paphlagonians of Pelops surrendered on the spot, even those* [on the island] *around which the dark waters of Billaeus break.*
ibid 2.774

Only one person could stop Hercules from pre-empting Alexander the Great and conquering the east a thousand years ahead of schedule, and that person was Eurystheus.

He sent messengers to inform Hercules that if he was done playing around, it was time to get back to his Labours. Since Hercules was near the country of the Amazon warrior women, that could be his next Labour. Hippolyte, queen of the Amazons was said to have a pretty girdle. The daughter of Eurystheus fancied it, so mighty Hercules, the conqueror of Phrygia, Bithynia and points east should immediately stop what he was doing and go get it.

Chapter 9

The Amazons, the Trojans, and the Coan incident

~~~~~~

'The Amazons, whose minds are set on war ...', says the poet Callimachus (*Hymn 3 to Artemis* 240) were favourites of the battle-god Ares, who had married Otrera, the first of the Amazon queens. The race of Amazons thus founded were formidable fighters who had gained the ungrudging respect of their opponents.

From the beginning the Amazons have been ruthless fighters. The spirit of the War God constantly inspires them so they labour as do men. They are in no way inferior - work has hardened their bodies, and given them great hearts which can achieve anything. They do not faint nor tremble at the knees, their queen is said to be a very daughter of the War God, and unequalled among women.
Quintus Smyrnaeus, *Fall of Troy* 1.618ff

The Amazons lived on the shores of the Black Sea, which the ancients called the Euxine. Indeed, according to Diodorus Siculus it was Hercules who gave that sea its name. The Amazons' city was called Themiscyra, and it was situated on the banks of the river Thermodon. There, we are told by Apollodorus [*Library* 2.5.9] the warlike Amazons 'cultivated the manly virtues'. It was the established practice of the era that unwanted children - mainly female - were killed through exposure. The Amazons did the contrary; 'If they gave birth to children ... they only raised the females. They pinched off their right breasts so they they might hurl javelins unimpeded, but kept the left for suckling their babes.' The Greeks believed that this latter practice gave the warriors their name - in Greek *a mazos* means 'without breast', though modern scholars have challenged this etymology.

111

The Amazons were as ferocious a bunch of warriors as any that Asia Minor had to offer. Eurystheus had good reason to hope that if Hercules was as diplomatic with Hippolyte in getting the Amazon queen's girdle as he had been with King Augeas in cleaning his stables, then another handy little war might break out. Furthermore, the Amazons were favourites of Ares, as the Stymphalian Birds had been. If Hercules kept picking on Ares, eventually the War God might retaliate. Hera, the mother of Ares, would be on hand to ensure that the wrath of the God would be directed at the right target - that is, at Hercules who did the deeds, not at Eurystheus who had ordered them. And indeed, this approach definitely had promise, for as will be seen, Ares was by now starting to view the activities of Hercules with an increasingly jaundiced eye.

Now that the precedent had been set with the Mares of Diomedes, Hercules was again allowed to bring volunteers to help him on this mission. Two of these volunteers were killed on the island of Paros, where the team made a stop-over. The killers were sons of King Minos of Crete. Hercules was already miffed with King Minos for the cool reception he had been given when he went to collect the Cretan Bull from that island (Labour #6). Consequently Hercules killed the offending sons of Minos on the spot and besieged their city until the survivors offered to make reparations.

Proceeding to Mysia in north-west Asia Minor, Hercules again took the opportunity to engage in some extra-curricular warfare. Finding that his host, King Lycus, was at war with a neighbouring kingdom, Hercules cheerfully threw himself into the combat. In the climatic battle of the war, he added the enemy king to the list of royalty he had already slain. This list already included King Augeas, the King of Orchomenus (probably) Diomedes of Thrace and the usurper king of Thebes. To these four, Hercules was to add at least another dozen royal corpses before he was done.

The land which Hercules won for King Lycus was used to found the city of Heraclea Pontica, which in later years fought Galacian invaders and was visited by Julius Caesar. Those wishing to follow in such distinguished footsteps should note that the city is today called Karadeniz Eregli, in Turkey's Zonguldak Province. ('Eregli' is a phonetic descendant of 'Heracles'.)

And so, finally, to the Amazon kingdom. Bad news like Hercules got about, so the adventurers were not completely unexpected when their ship put in at Themiscyra, (which later became the modern town of Terme, about 400 miles east along the Black Sea coast from Eregli/Heraclea.). Queen Hippolyte herself went down to the docks to enquire what Hercules wanted. The discovery that the hero wanted nothing more than her belt probably came as something as a relief to the warrior queen, who readily promised to hand it over. This speedy acquiescence thoroughly annoyed Hera, who as ever, was following the adventures of Hercules with malevolent interest. The girdle had been a gift to Hippolyte from her son Ares and it irked her that Hippolyte was prepared to so easily surrender it. Besides, what sort of challenge was it for Hercules to simply sail up, be given the object of his quest and sail away again? Was the man a hero or a glorified delivery boy?

There was yet the chance for mischief. Hippolyte and her retinue were as exotic to the adventurers as the Amazons were to them. Consequently Hercules' men crowded round gawking at the royal party, who stared right back. This close contact caused some unease among those Amazons watching from a distance. Unease turned to outright alarm and fury when Hera adopted the form of an Amazonian warrior and loudly announced that Hercules and his men planned to take not take just the belt, but also the queen whom it went around. Indeed, the kidnapping was already in progress, had the Amazons but eyes to see it. Without further prompting, the Amazons leapt to arms.

The first thing that Hercules knew of this development was when he saw the Amazons in full battle array, charging on horseback toward his men. Suspecting treachery, he killed the Amazonian queen as a precautionary measure (royal corpse #6), and then, remembering what he had come for, he quickly stripped off her girdle. Thereafter, even as they realized their initial mistake, the sight of their slain queen blinded the Amazons to reason.

The Amazons attacked with all their famed ferocity.

The Amazons would not listen to him, so in the end battle was joined, the mass of the Amazons against the followers of Heracles. But those with the greatest prestige among the Amazons went against Heracles himself, and they fought stubbornly against him.

First up was Aella the Swift, but she found that her opponent outmatched her in the speed which had given her name. Then came Philippis who was slain by a mortal blow at the very first strike of the duel. After her was Prothoê, seven times the victor in battlefield duels. When she fell, next in line was she

Unlike with the centaurs, Hercules did not make the Amazons extinct, but this was not through lack of effort on his part.

who was known as Eriboea. Eriboea claimed that her virtues were equal to any man and she needed no help in this conflict, but she was proven wrong.

Then came Celaeno, Eurybia, and Phoebê, hunting companions of [the goddess] *Artemis, whose spears had never before missed their mark. Shoulder-to-shoulder they stood, but their spears did not so much as graze their opponent and they were all cut down together. After them Deïaneira, Asteria and Marpê, and Tecmessa went down. Alcippê had taken a vow to die a virgin, and this vow she now fulfilled. The commander of the Amazons, Melanippê, for all her manly courage, next lost her supremacy.*

The most renowned of the Amazons were thus killed [or captured - Melanippê, for example survived]. *Heracles now turned on the rest of them and put them to flight. He cut down most of the fugitives, so that the race was*

114

exterminated.
Apollodorus *Library* 4.16.3ff

Were this report of Apollodorus accurate, this would be the second charge of genocide against the name of Hercules. (Or the third, if we count the Giants as well as the centaurs.). However, the accusation is ill-founded, for the Amazons did not fall into extinction. The warrior women lived to fight another day.

It is a fact that when the women from [the banks of the river] *Thermodon fled from Heracles, they sacrificed here to the Ephesian goddess* [Artemis], *as they knew the sanctuary of old.*
Pausanias on a shrine of Artemis *Guide to Greece* 7.2.7

The survivors of the struggle ended up taking refuge in Scythia, to the north of the Black Sea, for this is the place that several later myths describe as their homeland. Their population increased considerably within a generation, for they were soon numerous enough to mount a raid on Athens, and later fought on the side of Hector and his men against Achilles in the Trojan War. Hercules himself was partly responsible for the Amazonian raid on Athens, for the Amazons went to snatch back the captive warrior Antiopê whom Hercules had by then given as a present to his buddy Theseus. In recognition of her brave fight, Melanippê had been immediately freed by Hercules with just the price of her own girdle as a ransom (Apollodorus *ibid* 4.16.4). This made the Amazonian unique in being the only person to face Hercules in serious *mano-a-*(wo)*mano* combat who yet lived to tell the tale.

Prequel to the Trojan war

Ganymede is today a moon of Jupiter, but according to the ancient Greeks his orbit of the King of the Gods was once much closer. Young Ganymede was a prince of Troy, and like many of that breed, his physical beauty was outstanding. Jupiter/Zeus, who had sworn off mortal women after his tryst with Alcmene, found that he was attracted to human company nevertheless. When he saw young Ganymede hunting in the wilds of Phrygia in Asia Minor he immediately gave in to impulse, changed himself into the form of an eagle, and snatched the boy from his companions.

The hunter is carried aloft by the tawny wings, and the Garagara peaks fall as he rises past their level. Troy is lost in the haze below him, and his companions stand, sadly watching as the hounds grow hoarse with barking, chasing his shadow and baying at the clouds.
Statius *Thebaid* 1.549

Zeus later repented of his impetuous action and sent word to Troy, claiming that the young prince had become his cup-bearer (a position of honour which young squires held for the bronze-age kings of the day). Socrates and other Greek philosophers claimed that the boy remained inviolate, and that Zeus loved him only for his mind. Later Romans were more cynical, and one of the young prince's names ' - 'Catamite' – has since passed into modern English to mean a boy exploited for sexual purposes.

Zeus, King of the Gods, Lord of Olympus and abductor of young boys

By way of compensation Zeus sent his messenger Hermes to Laomedon, the king of Troy. Hermes brought with him a set of horses, not just magnificent in size and bearing, but so swift that they could run on water. The guilty conscience of Zeus did not stop there. When Apollo and Poseidon offended

Zeus in some way, he sent the pair to offer service to Laomedon. These two Gods appeared to the Trojan king as mortal heroes who offered to perform some service.

In acting as they did, the divine pair were intent on proving to Zeus that Laomedon was a scoundrel and undeserving of further sympathy for the loss of Ganymede. Laomedon set the pair to rebuilding his city's walls on a magnificent scale, and promised the labourers rewards to match. Nothing loath, Apollo and Poseidon put their backs into the task, and so were built 'the topless towers of Ilium' of which the poets sing. (Ilium was an alternative name for Troy, derived from Ilus, the city's founder.)

Laomedon felt very secure behind his new walls, which was unsurprising since they were so strong that neither men nor Gods could breach them. Therefore the king had no hesitation in proving Apollo and Poseidon right by reneging on his part of the bargain. The two Gods were thanked for their efforts and sent away with no further compensation. Later, Laomedon realized this was a mistake. For a start, Zeus wanted no more to do with a promise-breaker, and withdrew his protection from the city. 'Laomedon robbed the Gods by withholding the agreed payment,' confirms the poet Horace (*Carmina* 3.21)

This left Apollo and Poseidon free to wreak havoc. Thanks to its walls, the city of Troy was secure, but the city's fields were not. Poseidon 'the earth-shaker' was an earthquake God as well as Lord of the Sea. Now he used both attributes together to create tsunamis which flooded the cornfields of the Trojan plain. Apollo was God of the Arts, but also was Lord of the Flies, the God of Pestilence, and Laomedon swiftly discovered that walls, be they ever so strong, are no defence against microbes. With Poseidon's earthquakes and floods came a sea monster which ravaged the land. With his people starving and dying from plague, and a monster prowling outside the walls, it must have seemed to Laomedon that things could get no worse.

Then Hercules arrived.

At this point, Laomedon had resorted to the traditional means of getting rid of a sea monster. So just as her parents had done with Andromeda three generations previously, Laomedon chained his daughter Hesione to a rock in the hope that the monster would be sated by her royal blood and cease troubling the land thereafter. Hercules, the descendant of Perseus, could hardly pass by a maiden in distress just as great-grandmother had been.

Laomedon was constrained by necessity to deliver the maiden and to leave her, bound in chains, upon the shore. Heracles, when he had departed from the Argonauts and learned from the girl of her sudden change of fortune, tore away the chains from around her body. Then he went the city and offered to slay the monster for the king.
Diodorus Siculus 4.42.4

In the negotiations of Pursues with his future in-laws, the hero was set on marriage to Andromeda. However, Hercules had no more than a passing interest in the girl about to be sacrificed. Rather than a princess bride, Hercules wanted the horses of Zeus, the steeds so swift that they ran on water. Laomedon consulted the oracles and discovered that it was the will of the gods that if Hercules did indeed slay the monster, Poseidon and Apollo would altogether end their assault on Troy. Perhaps Apollo and Poseidon calculated that Laomedon now had Hercules, thus making further afflictions unnecessary. Sadly, the king was too short-sighted to realize this.

Laomedon accepted the proposal and promised to give as his reward the invincible mares, Heracles, they say, did then slay the monster
Diodorus Siculus 4.42.4

Once the sea monster had received such short shrift that no ancient poet has bothered to describe the killing, the king showed his total inability to learn from past experience. Once again the scoundrel reneged on his promise.

In his arrogant folly Laomedon with harsh words abused the man who had served him so well, and refused to hand over the mares for which he had travelled so far.
Homer *Iliad* 6.50

Hercules had outstanding business, namely a girdle to hand over, so he was forced to postpone his reckoning with the king. He set sail for Mycenae, but only after uttering a heart-felt threat to return at the earliest opportunity.

This was not Hercules' only parting shot on his return journey. At one of the harbours on the way to Mycenae, the hero was entertained by the local king, but repeatedly insulted by the king's brother, a man called Sarpedon. Sarpedon presumed on the fact that he was a son of Poseidon to save him from the anger of Hercules. As his ship sailed, Hercules noted the insolent individual on the beach. His ship had already left the dock, so Hercules was no longer bound to politeness by the rules of hospitality. Picking up his bow, he fired over the stern of the ship, killing Sarpedon on the spot.

There is some debate as to what happened next. All agree that, as arranged, Hercules handed over the Amazonian girdle to Eurystheus when he reached Mycenae and so completed his ninth Labour. Thereafter some versions of the epic have the Hercules putting Troy and King Laomedon on his 'to do' list for later while he proceeded directly to Labour number ten.

Other accounts, perhaps for narrative convenience, have Hercules immediately gathering a fleet and returning to Troy with vengence in mind. Here we follow the latter tradition, both for the narrative convenience which appealed to earlier authors and because Hercules was never a man to hold a grudge. When slighted he did not brood, but reacted immediately and usually lethally. So we can well believe that Hercules decided that his tenth Labour could wait until he had settled his dispute with the Trojan king.

Homer (*Iliad* 639) tells us that Hercules returned with just six ships, but by the time of Apollodorus the number has grown to 'Eighteen ships of fifty oars'. Since at this time the rowers were also warriors, this means that a band of nine hundred warriors hit the beaches outside Troy. Seeing how few men made up the host opposing him, Laomedon mounted a sally against their ships, as these were drawn up on the beach and lightly guarded. The king succeeded in killing Oicles, whom Hercules had left in charge of the ships, but came to grief when Hercules and his men came up in support.

Laomedon had not been expecting hostilities so soon, and at such short notice it proved impossible to muster a passable army. Gathering as many soldiers as he could he advanced against the ships, hoping that by burning them he could bring the war to an end. Oicles, the commander, came out to meet him, but when he was slain, his men rapidly pulled back in good order and put out to sea.

Laomedon then withdrew towards the city where he met the warriors of Heracles in battle. He was killed and most of the soldiers with him.
Diodorus Siculus *History* 4.32.4

After the creation of his latest royal corpse, Hercules drove the surviving Trojans behind the city walls to await the inevitable assault. With Hercules and the walls of Troy, irresistible force met immovable object. In this case, the classic conundrum was decided in favour of the irresistible force, mainly because the remnants of an already scanty Trojan army were too few to adequately man the walls. Inevitably, the main effort of the defenders was spent in blocking Hercules who chose to assault the strongest part of the wall, by the acropolis. This gave the other attackers an opportunity, which they made the most of. Here we get another glimpse of the unpleasant fellow Hercules was becoming.

[The hero] *Telamon was the first through the wall and into the city with Heracles close behind. When he saw that Telamon had entered before he had, Heracles was furious that someone had earned more glory than himself, so he drew his sword and rushed at him.*

Seeing his danger, Telamon began gathering whatever stones were immediately to hand. Heracles asked him what he was doing, and Telamon replied that he was constructing an altar to Heracles the Glorious Victor. Heracles thanked him ... and gave him Laomedon's daughter Hesione as a prize.
Apollodorus *Library* 2.6.4

A further development followed from this. Hercules 'sacked the city of Ilus, and laid waste to the streets,' reports Homer. In the process he slew all the remaining sons of Laomedon but one, a youth called Podarces. When Telamon was preparing to depart with Hesione, he said that she could pick any one of the captives from Troy as a companion. Hesione chose her brother Podarces, which Hercules readily consented to, for Podarces had been the only son to advise Laomedon to hand over the mares which he had promised.

However, Hercules insisted that as Podarces was now his prisoner and slave, so Hesione must ransom him. After a moment's hesitation, Hesione took the veil off her head and offered this as a token payment. This was accepted. Hesione chose to go voluntarily with Telamon (whom she later married), while the brother, now freed by her payment, chose not to accompany Hesione, but instead remained to rebuild Troy as the city's new king. However, as a permanent reminder of his debt to his sister, Podarces changed his name to Priam, which means 'paid for'.

Many years later Priam attempted to bring his sister back to Troy so the pair could spend their old age together. Therefore he sent his son Paris to Greece to negotiate Hesione's return. To everyone's dismay Paris lost the plot of his diplomatic mission. He returned instead with the young and beautiful Helen. But that, as they say is another story.

Meanwhile, Hercules, like Odysseus, found that conquering Troy was one thing, but sailing away from the place was another. Hera was even more furious with Hercules than she usually was, because she was the patron goddess of Troy, and Hercules, the 'glory of Hera' had just devastated her city. Therefore she conspired with Hypnos and the other Gods to put Zeus into a deep sleep, and while her husband slumbered, Hera had him bound with unbreakable cords.

Then, with Hercules' father temporarily out of the picture, Hera sent massive storms against the ships of Hercules and succeeded in sinking five of the six (we are back to the Homeric six ships at this point). Only the mighty efforts of Hercules kept his own ship afloat, but even that was a losing battle. But the sea nymph Thetis – who would later be the mother of Achilles - was on hand.

But you came, goddess, and freed Zeus from his bonds, when you had quickly called to high Olympus him of the hundred hands, whom the gods call Briareus.
Homer *Iliad* 1.398

Briareus of the hundred hands was one of the three god-monsters guarding the doors to Tartarus. His name means 'the strong one', and he proved it by snapping the supposedly unbreakable bonds like taffy. Once freed, Zeus demonstrated his bad temper to his wife in no uncertain terms. As an object lesson not to interfere directly in the affairs of Hercules, Zeus had Hera hung by her wrists from Mt Olympus. Just to make it clear that his feelings were really hurt, Zeus compounded the punishment by attaching anvils to each of Hera's ankles.

Meanwhile, back on the storm-tossed Aegean, Hercules was having an interesting time. A new narrator, the writer and philosopher Plutarch, takes up the story.

Why is it that among the people of Cos, the priest of Heracles at Antimacheia dons a woman's garb, and puts on a woman's head-dress before he begins the sacrifice?

Because:

Heracles, sailing with his six ships from Troy, ran into a storm. His other ships were destroyed and he, on the only one remaining, was driven before the gale to [the island of] Cos. He was cast ashore at the Laceter, as the place is called, and saved nothing from the shipwreck but his arms and his men. Coming across upon some sheep he asked the shepherd for one ram. This shepherd, whose name was Antagoras, was in the prime of bodily strength, and he challenged Heracles to wrestle with him. If Heracles could throw him, he would win the ram. And when Heracles grappled with him, the Meropes came to the aid of Antagoras.

Wrestling in heroic Greece was a serious and often fatal business
Detail from a black-figure wine cup c.500 BC Metropolitan Museum of Art, New York

As an aside, in the people of 21st century Cos have recently unveiled a statue on the site to commemorate this wrestling match. There was no winner, as the bout was interrupted by the Meropes. These were the local people, who seeing their hero Antagoras locked in combat with a stranger, leapt to the conclusion that the newcomers were pirates, and Hercules and his men were set on stealing their sheep.

The Greeks hurried to help Heracles, and things soon developed into a mighty battle.

Now it should be remembered that Hercules was already exhausted after an uncounted time spent keeping his ship afloat through a major storm. Furthermore, he and his men were greatly outnumbered.

In the struggle it is said that Heracles was exhausted and outnumbered by a multitude of adversaries. So he fled to the house of a Thracian woman and there disguised himself in feminine garb. Thus he managed to escape detection.

This was none too surprising. The Coans were now up to speed on whom they were fighting, and their search was for the conqueror of Troy, the slayer of the Hydra and the vanquisher of the centaur race. They failed to associate this man with the over-muscled transvestite lurking behind a foreign woman's couch, and the search passed Hercules by. Naturally enough Hercules neither forgot nor forgave. But he was prepared to admit that he had been beaten fair and square, and so reined in his natural vindictiveness.

Later, he overcame the Meropes in another encounter ('He forced his way in and took the city by night, and slew the king, Eurypylus' says Diodorus Siculus 2.7.1 of the creation of royal corpse #8). *After he had been purified, he married Chalciopê and assumed a gay-coloured raiment. This is why the priest sacrifices on the spot where that first battle was fought, and this is why Coan bridegrooms wear woman's clothes when they welcome their brides.*
Plutarch *Greek Inquiries* 58

Chapter 10

The Peripatetic Hero – Hercules at the ends of the Earth

If two Labours had not been disqualified, Hercules would have now been on his last labour. One can understand that Eurystheus was uncomfortable with this fact. As the now deceased kings Augeas and Laomedon could testify, Hercules cherished his vendettas and liked to pay back wrongs with interest. It will be remembered that the Labours were conceived as expiation for the killing of what Hercules had wrongly imagined to be Eurystheus and his sons. There was no reason why, once the Labours were complete, that Hercules should not pick up right where he had left off almost a decade previously and resume his feud with the kin of Pelops by killing off Eurystheus, that family's most outstanding member., and possibly his children too.

Actually, there was one reason, and this is best illustrated by an ancient statue which can still be viewed today. This is the 'Farnese Hercules'. Ancient as this statue is - it originally stood at the Baths of Caracalla in Rome - it is a copy of one more ancient still, the bronze original being probably made by the sculptor Lysippos in the fourth century BC. The statue is now in the National Archaeological Museum in Naples, despite a determined effort by Napoleon to steal it for his Italian collection in the Louvre.

We see Hercules in a rare moment of introspection. The classic motifs are present - the club, the lion-skin cloak, the huge and heavily-muscled body - but the dynamism which pervades both the story of Hercules and the sculpture of the period are both missing. Hercules has taken off his invincible cloak and draped it over his club. He is vulnerable, both in the sense that his cloak no longer protects him, and in the sense that he has for a moment dropped the persona of an invincible super-hero. Even the club which the lion-skin mostly covers is not used as a weapon, but as a crutch. The head of the club rests on a rock, and Hercules has the other end under his shoulder, propping himself up as he leans upon it. The other shoulder droops, as does the head of the mighty hero. His eyes are downcast, and the pose expresses bone-deep weariness. We see that Hercules is no longer a young man, or even in the prime of life.

The hero is at a crossroads. He has killed numerous monsters and even more human foes. His reputation among men is secure, but his family is dead by his own hand. Perhaps even now he is aware of the monster he must face in later life, a creature more savage and insidious than any of the comic-book creatures he has slain so far. That monster is within him, ever less patient of the demands of lesser men and the constraints of civilized behaviour. Hercules knows that whatever he wants he can take. None can stop him but himself, and stop himself he must, or he will become like Typhon or the Nemean Lion, just another monster to match any that have gone before.

The Farnese Hercules
Museo Archeologico Nazionale Naples

The weary Hercules has his brow furrowed as he asks himself how much longer he can keep on, for how many more years he must show himself to the world as a tireless, unstoppable hero. When the inevitable mistake or misjudgement happens, what nightmare of tentacles and teeth will eventually bring him down, with the malice of Hera waiting, spider-patient to ensure he never gets up again? And if he survives, what kind of man will he be? Himself a monster, or a burned-out wreck living in the shadow of his own reputation?

It is in this self-doubt and weariness that Eurystheus might have hoped for his salvation. Hercules might kill him once the Labours were complete. On the other hand, Hercules might be simply too tired to make the effort. Therefore, if signs of strain were showing, the best thing Eurystheus could do was to focus less on the sheer lethality of the Labours and concentrate on making the remainder as physically and spiritually demanding as possible. So when Hercules returned to Mycenae, weary and jaded from his exertions in Asia Minor, Eurystheus cheerfully announced that the next adventure lay beyond the borders of the known world.

The Labour itself was straightforward, and did not explicitly require Hercules to kill anyone or anything. Hercules had merely to proceed to Gadira and there obtain the cattle of Geryon and bring them back to Mycenae. Naturally enough, Geryon was a fearsome monster who might be expected to object to the loss of his cattle, but this was not the first of Hercules' problems in fulfilling his task. The initial challenge was simply finding where Gadira was.

Diligent inquiries by the hero produced the opinion Gadira was on an island, and that island lay just beyond where a mighty river flowed through a narrow strait. There was an obvious choice, and this lay to the north-east where the River Danube flows into the Black Sea. Here, claim some who study the myths, lay the original locality of this Labour, which certainly explains the Scythian connection which we shall come to in due course. However, by the time the myths came to be written down, Gadira had moved. The site was now still more distant and exotic – as the poet Pindar says, 'Beyond Gadira towards the western darkness there is no passage. Turn back the sails and strike for the European mainland' (*Nemean Odes* 4.69). In short, Gadira lay in the western Ocean beyond the shores of the Mediterranean, not far from the city

126

sometimes believed to have taken its name; Gades, or Cadiz in modern Spain.

However, unlike its modern namesake on the European mainland, legendary Gadira was believed to be on an island, Erytheia, the 'red island of the sunset'. The ancient geographer Strabo quotes the even more ancient poet Stesikhorus while grappling with the geographical confusion surrounding so far-off a location

The ancient writers seem to call the [river] *Baetis the Tartessos. Gades is Gadira and the nearby island Erytheia. This, it is supposed, is why Stesikhoros should say of Geryon's herdman that he was born 'almost opposite famous Erytheia'*
Strabo *Geography* 3.2.11

Listeners to the myths knew the challenge of a mission beyond the shores of the Mediterranean, because just getting there was a difficult feat. The inland sea loses water through evaporation which is replaced by a current which flows in from the Atlantic on the surface, thus also replacing water which flows out through a cold undersea current on the ocean floor. So any ship trying to sail to Gades needs to maintain the speed of a brisk jog on land just to stay still against the prevailing current.

Since Hercules had now found his destination, distant as it was, he had perforce to set out on his mission. Step One took him to the isle of Crete, a way station on Hercules' journey to Africa, where the plan was to travel westward along the north African littoral. While in Crete, Hercules decided to clear the island of harmful beasts. So as a tribute to his father Zeus (who was raised on Crete) Hercules killed off all the poisonous snakes, wolves, bears and other predators which were such a nuisance on the mainland.

He came to Crete, having decided to set of from that island, which is exceptionally well-placed for expeditions to any part of the known world. Out of gratitude to the natives for the magnificent honours he received from the Cretans and for the glory of the place which was the birthplace and early home of Zeus, he cleansed the island of the wild beasts which infested it. And this is why ever since not a single wild animal, not a bear, or wolf, or serpent, or any thing of this sort is to be found on the island.
Diodorus Siculus *History* 4.17.3

Some beasts might have sneaked back over the centuries, for the apostle Paul is also credited with later achieving the same feat of wildlife suppression. More recently modern archaeologists and zoologists have combined in a spoilsport way to argue that in fact almost all the animal life on Crete was imported by humans, and the island is free of wolves, bears and so on because no-one had any reason to attempt the difficult feat of importing them in the first place.

Be that as it may, Hercules proceeded to Africa. Libya was the first to feel the shock of his arrival. The local giant Antaeus was in the habit of challenging newcomers to the land to a wrestling match and then killing off the losers after his inevitable victory. After winning his bout Hercules continued the tradition of killing the loser, and being in full kill mode, he proceeded to go through the country as he had through Crete.

'He subdued Libya, which was full of wild animals ... which had infested the land to the point of making it uninhabitable. Thereafter he enabled it [Libya] *to be cultivated and as prosperous as anywhere else.*
Diodorus Siculus *History* 4.17.4 *passim*

This was Hercules fulfilling the role we was born for. While he was himself more than somewhat uncivilized, Hercules was the agent of Zeus, the God of Order. Once the chaos had subsided in the wake of the hero's passage, the population of the area found themselves able to pick up their lives without the monsters, thuggish giants and other agents of chaos who had previously blighted their existence. The cleansing of Libya took Hercules to the borders of Egypt, with a quick side-trip into that country to pile up royal corpse #8, apparently by way of objection to the Egyptian King Busiris' habit of killing all visitors who trespassed into his land. Returning to Libya, Hercules founded the city of Hecatompylon (literally 'of the hundred gates'- not to be confused with the more famous city of the same name in Persia). Then after a whirlwind few months sorting out the eastern African littoral, Hercules struck out west-ward across the desert to complete his original mission.

At this point a hitherto undiscovered flaw in his travel plans became apparent. The desert was hot, and as a big fellow in a lion-skin cloak, Hercules suffered from the heat more than most. Day after day he trudged through the sands with the flaming chariot of the Sun God Helios above, yet almost close enough to singe his hair. The lack of self-control which was increasingly a feature of Hercules' character quickly came to the fore, and when Helios next made a low pass over his head, the frustrated hero let loose a shot at the chariot with his bow.

Taking pot shots at the Gods was not a recommended survival technique in the world of myth, but Helios both liked Hercules and - for reasons we need not go into here - had something of a grudge against Hera. So out of admiration for the audacity of Hercules' defiance, Helios gave the hero a huge golden goblet which would allow him to complete his travels by sea. (It was this goblet which Helios usually used to return to the east in time for his next day's transit of the sky. What alternative transport he used while Hercules had his goblet is unrecorded.) Hercules travelling in this novel craft was later a popular theme with painters of pottery, particularly cups which depict Hercules in his goblet, clutching bow and club as he peers hopefully across the waves toward his destination.

Hercules at sea
Sketch from a Red-figure Kylix drinking cup in the Vatican Museum

There is some confusion as to what the hero did at the juncture of the Mediterranean and the Atlantic. By some accounts - e.g. Apollodorus - Hercules merely left two mountains on either side of the strait to commemorate his passage beyond the shores of civilization. The mountains had been there already, but were of different sizes, so Hercules simply evened them up, taking the excess from one mountain and dumping it on the other.

By another account, when Hercules wanted to sail into the Atlantic he discovered that the Mediterranean had no access to that ocean. So the hero promptly dug out the strait, and piled the soil and rock from the excavation on either side, creating what was known throughout the remainder of antiquity as the 'Pillars of Hercules' - the modern Rock of Gibraltar and the Moroccan Jebel Musa. There is also a credulity-stretching final version of the tale. By this account Mediterranean Sea and Atlantic Ocean were already linked, but Hercules decided that the strait was in fact too wide to properly deserve that name, so he pulled the continents of Africa and Europe somewhat closer together. As a result the passage between the seas became narrow enough to block the entry of the sea monsters which Poseidon was fond of inflicting on mankind. 'In this matter,' comments Diodorus Siculus resignedly, 'every man may think as he pleases'.

Having travelled beyond the bounds of the known world and across the ocean to the lands of the sunset, Hercules made landfall at Mt Abas, on the mysterious isle of Erytheia. His arrival was immediately noticed by Orthrus, the watchdog whom Geryon had set to guard his herd. As one might expect, Orthrus was no ordinary hound, but the two-headed offspring of the fearsome Typhon (pp 45, 54 etc) and the loathsome serpent-woman Echidna. This made the watchdog a full brother of the mighty Nemean Lion which Hercules had slain in his first Labour, as the Lion was also the child of Typhon and Echidna (a third member of this unholy little family was the man-killing Theban sphinx, later slain by Oedipus). However, Orthrus was not as formidable as his leonine sibling had been, and in the years since then, constant practice at deadly confrontations had made Hercules a great deal more formidable.

Therefore the battle between hero and watchdog was limited to a few snarls followed by a meaty crunch as Hercules' olive-tree club dispatched Orthrus to the underworld.

Before him, slain, lay that most murderous hound Orthrus, in his fury and might like Cerberus his brother-hound.
Quintus Smyrnaeus, *The Fall of Troy* 6.278

Nevertheless, the commotion was enough to rouse Eurytion, the herdsman. He made an ill-advised effort to aid his dog, and swiftly shared the same fate at the business end of Hercules' club. It should be noted that both herdsman and hound were, by modern standards, innocent victims of a homicidal cattle rustler from the sea. Certainly dog and owner were different physically from the usual forms of their respective species, but there is no record that either individual posed a threat to anyone, and a physical difference is no reason for murder. We, conditioned by the terms of the narrative, see the heroic Hercules doing battle with monsters in exotic lands far beyond the horizon. To the natives of those exotic lands, it is Hercules who was the monster, come to pillage and kill without compassion or excuse.

In the view of his own time, Hercules cannot be judged quite so harshly. In the era of myth, any seafarer was essentially a pirate or freebooter should the opportunity present itself. This fact is partly reflected by reality, as shown by the fact that many cities founded at this time are slightly set back from the sea. Both Athens and Rome, for example, were not port cities, but a few kilometres inland and linked to Pireaus and Ostia respectively. These ports dealt with maritime trade, but in the event of a large-scale pirate attack the main cities were insulated from harm. (Ostia was sacked by pirates as late as 68 BC, so this was indeed a reasonable precaution.)

It was generally considered to be the task of those ashore to present defences sufficiently formidable to convert would-be pirates into the friendlier role of traders. If the defenders failed in this task, then those on the ships were free to indulge in looting and pillage without attracting general opprobrium, however strongly those on the spot might disagree. Neither Odysseus nor 'pious' Aeneas were above doing a bit of freelance raiding on their travels, so perhaps we cannot judge Hercules too severely. As even Plato remarked philosophically of Hercules' conduct.

He took the cattle. They were neither purchased from Geryon nor given by him. [Hercules] *regarding it as the natural right of anyone superior or*

131

stronger to posses himself of the cows or any other property of the inferior or weak.
Plato *Gorgias* 484b

Of course, Geryon felt differently. The Lord of the Underworld, Hades, also pastured his cattle on the same island. The herdsman of Hades was a man called Menotes, and it was he who rushed to Geryon with the news that his herdsman and hound had been slain, and even now his cattle were being stolen away. Geryon was himself a formidable creature who must have felt that he had a chance against pillaging Hercules. A Giant, he was the grandson of the God Oceanus and the son of Chrysaor, the 'Golden Sword', brother of Pegasus. Like his father, Geryon was winged, and from the waist upward, he had three bodies. These 'wielded three spears in his [right] hands; while shields protruded from the three on the left. Shaking the three crests [on his three helmets], he advanced, looking like Ares in his might'.

This description comes from a fragment of the play *The Heracleidae* by the Athenian playwright Aeschylus. The ancients also had the full story of the encounter from a an epic poem by the writer Stesikhorus. His *Geryoneis* is now almost entirely lost, but enough fragments remain for us to piece together much of the story.

Seeing Geryon determined to confront Hercules, the herdsman Menotes begged him to reconsider.

'Think of [your father] Chrysaor beloved of Ares, and of Callirhoe, your mother. (fr S10)

As we know from past experience, anything 'beloved of Ares' was likely to receive unsympathetic treatment from Hercules who seemed to positively delight in harming things sacred to the War God, the son of Hera, his divine tormentor. In any case, when the pleas of Menotes went unheeded, the herdsman brought the mother Callirhoe herself to plead with her son.

Heracles was already coming, so she addressed him 'Victory goes to the strongest ... obey me my son.' (fr S12)

Geryon replied

Do not try to chill my manly heart with talk of death ... if my birth makes me immortal then henceforth my life shall be spent on Olympus, and [if I die] *this is better than to endure those who will reproach me that I simply watched my cattle driven away from their byres. ... It is nobler to suffer whatever is fated than to flee death and shower disgrace on my sons and all of my line thereafter. I am Chrysaor's son! May* [my death] *not be the wish of the blessed gods.* (fr S11)

Evidently this reminded Callirhoe to take her case to the court of Zeus, and she fled in an instant to Olympus where the Gods were already assembled. Callirhoe was making progress on behalf of her son, especially with Poseidon. Then Athena intervened for Hercules, her protégé.

[None] *remained on the side on Zeus, the King of All. Then spoke grey-eyed Athena to her stubborn uncle, the Lord of Horses. 'Come now, bring to mind that you gave a promise* [not to save] *Geryon from death.'* (fr S14)

Meanwhile, back on Erytheia ...

After a mental debate, it seemed better to Heracles ... to fight from ambush against one so mighty. ... Thus he devised the bitter destruction. ... [An arrow] *smeared with gall and blood from the dappled neck of the man-killing Hydra in its agony, he cunningly and silently fired into his* [opponent's] *forehead. Guided by the Gods it sliced through flesh and bone running straight and true through the crown of his head. Then gushed the blood on to limb and breastplate, and Geryon drooped his head sideways, like a tender poppy which mars its beauty by suddenly shedding the petals on one side.* (fr S15)

'Thus', remarks the poet Vergil in the epic *Aeneid*, 'was Geryon slain. Three was the Giant, who thrice lived in vain'. (*Aeneid* bk 8)

Having won his victory and possessed himself of the cattle, Hercules might have hoped that his Labour was largely complete. In fact it was just beginning. Getting to the isle of Erytheia had been a challenge for one man travelling alone. Since getting the cattle across the dry wastes of the Libyan desert was out of the question, Hercules would have to travel overland through western Europe. This was a wild, uncivilized area, packed with monsters and tribes which all shared a taste for steak.

The journey started well enough. Hercules packed the cattle into the golden bowl of Helios and made landfall at Tartessos on the European mainland. Returning the his craft to the Sun God, Hercules and his herd proceeded along the coast.

He then passed through the country of the Iberians. Because he was honoured by one of the native kings, a man of great piety and justice, Heracles presented the king with some of the cattle. The king accepted them, but dedicated them all to Heracles. Every year he sacrificed to Heracles the most magnificent bull of that herd. And even today that herd is still maintained in Iberia and the cattle remain sacred to Heracles.
Diodorus Siculus *History* 4.18.3

The trip through Gaul was equally uneventful, and mainly notable for a romance with the Gallic princess Galata (making the pair ancestors of the warrior race of the Galatians, to whom St Paul later wrote one of his epistles), and the subsequent foundation of the fortress-city of Alesia where in historical times the Gallic Wars of Julius Caesar came to an end with the successful siege and surrender of the city.

The first problem on the homeward leg of the mission came in Liguria, that area of modern Italy where Genoa now stands. In fact part of the problem was simply getting the cattle to the coastal plain. In the end Hercules ended up driving a road through the Alps. In Liguria, two sons of Poseidon, Albion and Dercynus there decided to relieve Hercules of the burden of taking the cattle any further.

Given how he had come by the cattle, Hercules could hardly object to others attempting to take them from him in the same manner. However, his olive-tree club made the case for retaining possession more powerfully than any lawyer. The deaths of their two heroes offended the Ligurians who descended on Hercules in a body. This Prometheus had foreseen;

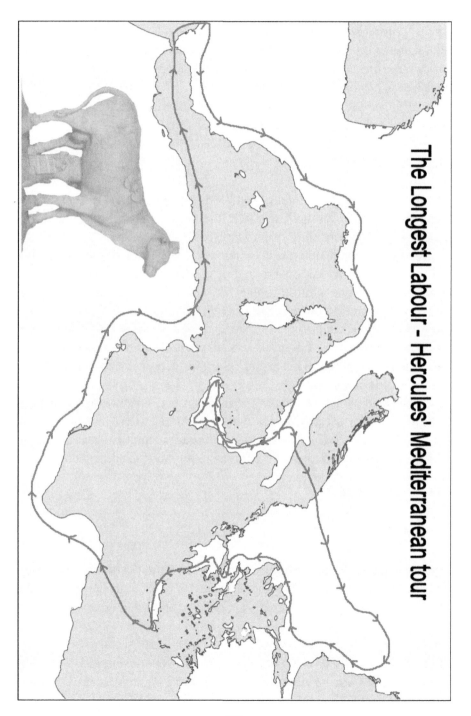

The Longest Labour - Hercules' Mediterranean tour

You will encounter the fearless host of the Ligurians
And tough as you are, you will find little fault with their war-making
You will see that your arrows will run out, and nor can you pluck
Stones from the soft muddy ground.
But seeing you in trouble, your father [Zeus] will pity you
And from a cloud will rain stones enough to darken the land
with these you will pelt the Ligurian host, and repel them with ease.
Aeschylus *Prometheus Unbound* fr 199

A later philosopher, Posidonius, (c. 130-55 BC) objected to the unnecessary duplication of labour in this event. Why did Zeus not simply drop the stones on top of the Ligurians since that was where Hercules was going to throw the things anyway? On the other hand, notes Strabo, the later geographer, why not kill Paris while he was en route from Troy, so that he never met Helen, which would save everyone a lot of trouble? The Gods worked in mysterious ways. Strabo was interested in the matter because he needed to explain why the plain in question was littered with stones (and remains so in Liguria to this day. The site was once a prehistoric flood plain of the river Rhone, and the unromantic may prefer to believe that the river deposited the stones when it regularly burst its banks.)

From Liguria south down the Italian peninsula, since it was the plan of Hercules to swim his herd across the Adriatic from where modern Brindisi now stands. In central Italy there was a further attempt to steal the cattle. Another Diodorus, Diodorus of Halicarnassus tells the full tale.

The legendary account of the arrival of Heracles is as follows. Being commanded by Eurystheus to drive Geryon's cattle from Erytheia to Argos, ... [Hercules] *came to the neighbourhood of Pallatium.*

This Pallatium is the first recorded settlement on the hill which still derives from that name today - the Palatine in Rome. However, at this point Pallatium was a village, and most of the area was woodland and wilderness.

Finding the grass excellent for his cattle, he [Hercules] *put them them to graze, and being weary, he lay down and was overwhelmed by sleep. There was a bandit called Cacus who lived thereabouts. When he saw the cattle grazing unguarded, he was seized with a desire to possess them. However, Heracles lay nearby asleep, and driving away the herd was sure to waken him. So took just a few of the cattle and concealed them in his hide-out in a nearby cave. He dragged each cow backwards by the tail so that the tracks led in exactly the opposite direction to which the cattle had actually gone.*

This shows our Cacus to be a classical scholar of sorts for exactly the same trick was pulled by the young Hermes when he stole the cattle of Apollo. It did not work for Hermes and it did not work for Cacus.

Heracles was not sure what to do next, so he had the bright idea of driving his cattle past the cave. When the cattle inside heard the lowing and smelled the rest of the herd, they bellowed to them in their turn, and so the theft was discovered. With his crime brought to light, Cacus called for his fellow herdsmen to come to his defence, but Heracles killed him with a blow of his club and took back his cattle.
Diodorus of Halicarnassus *Roman Antiquities* 1.39

The poet Vergil dedicates a goodly chunk of book eight of his epic *Aeneid* to this struggle in verses too long to repeat here, but this sample might give a flavour of the full version.

The monster Cacus, more than half a beast,
This cave, hidden from the sun, possessed
A floor befouled with human gore;
Heads, and mangled limbs, hung at the door.

The hero stood with planted feet, and, from the right,
Tugged the solid stone with all his might.
And heaved at the foundations of the rock
Which fast gave way before the shock.

The monster, spewing fruitless flames, he found
He choked his throat; wrung his neck around,
And in a knot those crippled limbs he bound.

From their sockets he tore his burning eyes
Then collapsed and still the breathless robber lies.
Aeneid bk 8 *passim*

With Cacus blinded, tied in a knot and eventually slain, our hero was free to resume his journey. However, he had passed through the site where Rome was later founded, and the Romans were not going to let that passage go unremarked. By their later legends the hero sacrificed a calf to Zeus to celebrate the reunification of his herd. He also erected a small temple both in thanksgiving and in expiation of the killing of Cacus. According to the *Roman Antiquities* of Diodorus of Halicarnassus both the temple of Jupiter the Discoverer and the tradition of the sacrifices there still remained in his own time, a thousand years later - though by then the expanding city of Rome had enveloped the original rural field. (The temple was eventually destroyed in the Great Fire of Rome in Nero's time.)

However, the shrine built by grateful locals to commemorate the removal of Cacus survived, and still survives. Even today, a visitor to the forum Boarium ('the cattle forum') in Rome can see the little round temple built in the Greek style which now stands on that site. Called the temple of Hercules the Victor, the temple was rebuilt in the second century BC as the earliest marble temple in Rome.

The Temple of Hercules Victor as it stands today beside the Tiber in Rome

Chapter 11

Of cows and apples

Over the months that he spent herding the cows of Geryon, Hercules got to know individual animals well enough to give them names. One particular bull was more trouble than it was worth, as the beast was of an independent mind and kept breaking away from the herd, forcing the exasperated Hercules to travel far and wide to round up the wilful creature. The bull's name was Italus, and the area it covered in its ramblings subsequently came to be called Italy. While both Aristotle and the great Greek historian Thucydides are happy to agree with this etymology, modern historians concur only on the point that the word *(v)italus* meant 'cow', 'calf', or 'cattle' in a number of ancient languages on the peninsula.

Perhaps the most spectacular break for freedom made by the bull Italus came at Rhegium in south Italy. This time the beast reached the sea, and undeterred by the expanse of water, swam all the way to Sicily. Hercules repeated the feat which he had performed with the Cretan Bull almost a decade previously, and holding the horn of one of his other bulls, he swam with the herd to Sicily in pursuit. Once on the island he discovered that Italus had strayed into the herds of King Eryx, a son of Aphrodite (or by other accounts, a child of Poseidon). When Hercules demanded his bull back, King Eryx proposed a wrestling match and a wager.

The contest of the rivals was not without penalty to the loser, for Hercules would have to give up his cattle, and if he lost, Eryx was to hand over his kingdom. At first Eryx disagreed with the conditions, complaining that the cattle were of far less value than his kingdom. In answer Hercules showed that by losing the cattle [his Labour would fail and] *he would lose his chance of*

immortality. Thereafter Eryx agreed to the terms, and lost both the wrestling match and his land.
Diodorus Siculus 4.23.2

The fate of his kingdom was not particularly relevant to ex-King Eryx, for he perished in the contest, to become Hercules' royal corpse #12. Thus our hero found himself in possession of a kingdom he could not hold and did not need, so he turned the land over to its people and told them to hold it in trust for his descendants. These descendants did in fact return to Sicily to 'reclaim' their ancestral inheritance, for much of the island was later settled by colonists from Sparta. (The Spartans considered Hercules their ancestor, and in his honour named one of their early Sicilian settlements Heraclea.)

On this, the most peripatetic of his adventures, our hero was still in no hurry to go home. He seems to have failed to recognize that Sicily was an island, for he went all around the coastline looking for passage north or east. When that passage failed to materialize he took out his frustration on the local tribe of the Sicels by conquering them, and then headed back to the strait.

During his time in Sicily he was assured that Zeus still favoured him, because the nymphs created a series of hot springs to soothe his weary bones at each place he stopped. (The later Greeks and Romans likewise availed themselves of these springs on their own journeys.) Hercules also noted that at one point his cattle left footprints in solid rock, and he took this as further proof of his pending immortality. The location of these footprints - which would be of great interest to modern palaeontologists - was known to the ancients but is lost today.

The crossing to Greece was a fairly straightforward affair, though wrestling Hercules for his cattle seems to have become a minor contemporary sport among the more suicidal members of the Italian aristocracy. Kings were especially enthusiastic participants and by the time he reached the Greek mainland, the Herculean body-count of crowned corpses had reached #15. Once he had arrived in Greece, Hercules required only a short and uneventful trip to the court of Eurystheus. However, Hera was not prepared to see yet another of the few remaining Labours successfully accomplished. As Hercules was gathering his cattle for a successful arrival, the Goddess sent a massive gadfly to torment the herd. Harried by the stinging fly, the maddened cattle fled north and east. By the time the fly gave up, the cattle were scattered in the wild lands on the western borders of the Black Sea. It appeared that Hercules would have to go to Thrace for his cattle after all.

The world's first historian, Herodotus of Halicarnassus, now takes up the story.

Thus Heracles came to the land now called Scythia. As he came thence, so also came a storm together with icy cold. So he drew his lion's skin over himself and went to sleep. Meanwhile the mares which pulled his chariot mysteriously disappeared as they were feeding. When Heracles awoke he searched for them over the whole land.

At last he came to the region called Hylaia. There in a cave he found a bipartite creature formed by the union of a young woman and a serpent. From the buttocks upwards the body was that of a woman, but her lower parts were those of a snake. Having seen and been amazed by her, Heracles asked if she had seen any mares straying thereabouts. She said that she herself had the mares, and was keeping them until Heracles lay with her. Heracles did so, wanting to retrieve his horses. This went on for some time, with her trying to put off giving back the mares and keep Heracles with her for as long as possible, while he on the other hand wanted to get the mares and go.

When she finally returned the mares, she said, 'I saved these for you when they came to me, and have been rewarded for doing so, for I will have three sons by you. So tell me what must I do with these when they grow to manhood. Shall I settle them here, on the lands which I rule, or send them off to you?'

They say that he replied, 'When the boys are men, this is precisely what you should do. Whichever of them can bend this bow as I am now doing and whoever can wear this belt, make him settle upon this land. Those that fail, send them away - that way you will enjoy what you have, and do as I wish.'

Then he handed over one of his bows (for they say that until then Heracles usually carried a spare) and gave her both bow and belt, which latter at the end of its clasp had a golden cup. That done, he departed. When her sons had been born and grown into men ... she did as instructed. ... Skythes, the youngest of them, performed the task and it was he who remained in the land. From Skythes, the son of Heracles, the kings of the Scythians are descended. They

also say that it is for this reason that the Scythians even to this day wear cups attached to their belts.
The History of Herodotus 4.8-10

Having collected his mares and founded yet another warrior race, Hercules got back to rounding up his cattle. After a year he had enough - both enough cattle and enough of collecting them. Leaving the remainder to run wild, Hercules drove those cattle he had back toward Greece. Mulishly stubborn, Hera raised the river Strymon in flood against him, but Hercules merely responded by raising the river bed by piling it with rocks. The tiff between Goddess and hero was later used to explain why a formerly navigable river had become impassable almost overnight. (An avalanche would have had the same effect, but would be unromantically mundane.)

Yet again, on his southward journey through Greece, Hercules attracted a horde of fans who accompanied him on his journey. Yet Hercules was dangerous company, and this was shown again when the procession arrived at the Isthmus of Corinth. At this time, the Isthmus was occupied by a giant called Alcyoneus. This is almost certainly a relative of the cattle-stealing Alcyoneus who kicked off the Gigantomachy (p.90ff), and was consequently killed by Hercules. This Alcyoneus had the same love of cattle and a huge dislike of the hero. When the column of travellers led by Hercules came within range, the Giant picked up two massive rocks and hurled them, one rock at Hercules and the other at his followers.

That great warrior, the terrible Giant, Alcyoneus, who armed only with rocks, flattened twelve four-horse chariots and twice that number of the men who stood on them, every one a proud knight ...
Pindar Nemean Ode 4

The rock hurled at Hercules was met with a swing of the hero's mighty club, and batted aside. There was to be no third strike in this bout of major-league mythological baseball, because thereafter Hercules shifted from club to bow 'and spared no strength as he let loose the deep music of his bowstring' (Pindar again). The arrow thus propelled brought about the end of both

Alcyoneus and his seven daughters, since the women threw themselves into the sea at the news of their father's death.

There were several consequences of this, the last dramatic event in the longest of Hercules' Labours. Firstly the massive rock thrown by Alcyoneus remained on the Isthmus, a landmark to travellers for the remainder of antiquity. Secondly, the giant's suicidal daughters did not die, because the sea nymph Amphitrite transformed the daughters into kingfishers (*Alcyon* in Greek). Aeolus, God of the Winds later made the sea calm for two weeks every winter so the waves would not crush the eggs which the birds laid on the beach. So from a violent event near Corinth comes the modern expression for days of calm and peace during tough times - our Halcyon Days. Finally, the fact that Hercules killed two cattle-rustling Giants with the same name means that when archaeologists unearth a vase or cup showing Hercules, a dead Giant and cattle (as archaeologists are wont to do occasionally) we today have no idea whether the Gigantomachy or the tenth Labour is there depicted.

The final obstacle overcome, Hercules was now able to complete the Labour which had taken him so many years. As ever, Eurystheus accepted Hercules' success ungraciously and immediately sacrificed the cattle to Hera, his partner in the anti-Hercules project.

Only two Labours remained, so Eurystheus had much to ponder upon. By his count, the tenth Labour had been a roaring success. It had taken several years to complete, it had removed Hercules from Greece for most of that time, and all the while the hero had been in mortal peril to a greater or lesser extent. The only drawback from Eurystheus' jaundiced viewpoint was that the task had not actually proven fatal, despite sporting attempts by the like of Alcyoneus. So perhaps the eleventh Labour should be something along the same lines, but with extra monsters?

Eurystheus was well aware that he had only two further tasks to assign to Hercules, and even those two tasks were only on the books because of some nifty work with the fine print of the original assignments. When Hercules had been sent for the cattle of Geryon, he had been forced to spend considerable time searching for the legendary island on which the cattle lived. Very well, decided Eurystheus. Let Hercules go west again, this time to a land even more remote and mysterious. Just to add an element of difficulty to the challenge, Eurystheus selected a location where no mortal, not even the semi-divine son of Zeus could set foot. This was the Garden of the Hesperides.

The Garden of the Hesperides
Detail from a painting by Ricciardo Meacci (1856-1938)

To understand this garden and its mystic inhabitants we must shuttle back and forth in time for a few moments. We begin at the dawn of myth when matters were somewhat confused. At this time the Titans roamed the Earth and Zeus and the Olympian Gods had not yet come into their power. Among the Titans was one Atlas, by some accounts brother to that Prometheus who was, in the time of Hercules, still chained to a rock in the Caucasus mountains as a punishment from Zeus for giving fire to humanity. Like his brother, Atlas was a scholar of some renown who specialized in astronomy and astrology. It was Atlas who identified and named Hesperus, the evening star (from whom we get our modern Vespers). So by conflation, Atlas became a sort of step-father to the children of Hesperus. These were the Hesperides, maidens of the sunset, and Goddesses of the Evening. 'Beyond glorious Ocean, on the frontier of Night where are found the clear-voiced Hesperides', says the poet Hesiod (*Theogony* 275).

The number and names of the Goddesses vary with the telling, sometimes three and sometimes four, but two of the names are already familiar in our saga. One of the originals was Medusa, beautiful as her sisters before being transformed to a hideous Gorgon by the vengeance of Athena. It will be remembered that it was on his return from slaying Medusa that Perseus saw the chained Andromeda and so began the line of Hercules. Another sister was Erytheia, 'the Red' who gave her name to the isle on which Geryon pastured his cattle.

The Goddesses - however many they were and howsoever they were called - lived far from mankind in the lands of the sunset. In particular they dwelt in a garden where they tended fruit trees which bore golden apples. These apples were no normal apples, for they were given to Hera when she married her brother Zeus. The nature of these apples has aroused considerable speculation. At the time oranges were unknown in the west, though they were just beginning to be cultivated in China. Some speculate that a trader had managed to obtain seeds and set himself a secluded orchard somewhere in the west (even today the Greeks call oranges 'Portugai') and there cultivated his 'golden apples'. Others dismiss this theory altogether. The golden apples, say these revisionists, are tomatoes. Now, while we today imagine the tomato as being fire-engine red, this was not always the case. The original tomatoes were a golden yellow when they were first imported into Europe, as their name in Italian 'pomodori' still signifies. ('Pomodori' literally translates as 'apples of gold'.) Even more suggestively, these first golden tomatoes were indeed imported from the lands beyond the sunset, for the original tomato comes from Peru, beyond the western ocean.

Some of these apples, be what they may, had left their sacred orchard just before Eurystheus decided to send Hercules off to get more. Aphrodite had 'borrowed' some to slow the virgin hero Atalanta when she ran a footrace against her prospective spouse. Atalanta was in the habit of killing those suitors who could not outrun her, so Aphrodite gave a promising candidate three golden apples. Every time Atalanta caught up with her swain, he dropped an apple, and fascinated, Atalanta slowed down to retrieve it.

Atalanta was a contemporary of Hercules, and indeed the pair were almost shipmates on the *Argo* when it set off to retrieve the Golden Fleece. However, at the last moment Jason had decided that a beautiful maiden with pronounced homicidal tendencies might be too disruptive for an otherwise all-male crew, so Atalanta's application to participate in the voyage was rejected. Nevertheless, the story of Atalanta's apples and the courtship race would have been well-known in Greece at the time, and perhaps it was this mention of the apples that got Eurystheus thinking.

Perhaps here we should also leap into the future, and the wedding of Thetis, the mother-to-be of the warrior hero Achilles. Uninvited to the wedding, the goddess Eris ('Discord') threw a golden apple into the crowd at the wedding feast. Inscribed 'For the fairest' this golden apple provoked a dispute between Hera, Aphrodite and Athena as to who was 'the fairest' whom the apple was for. This led to Paris of Troy adjudicating in favour of Aphrodite, getting the beautiful Helen as his reward and starting the entire Trojan War as a result.

This tale also means that Hercules had already come across one of the golden apples, for we know of his first meeting with the Apple of Discord. When on an unspecified adventure, Hercules came across this apple lying on a rock in a mountain pass. Idly the hero swung his club at it, expecting the result to be a satisfying crunch of shattered fruit. Instead the mighty club rebounded, and the apple remained there, if anything larger and healthier than before. Apples can't look smug, but this one was evidently trying. Provoked, Hercules gave the apple a mighty whack which simply made the thing even larger and glossier. Being Hercules, our hero proceeded to pound away at the apple until it was bigger than a house, and practically blocked the pass. At this point Athena noticed what her wayward protégé was up to and explained things to him. This golden apple would become the infamous Apple of Discord. The more you got violent with it, the larger it became. Ignore it, and eventually the apple would shrivel away.

These then, were the golden apples. These are not, incidentally, 'The Golden Apples of the Sun' as they are called by some writers of Herculean myth who should know better. Those apples belong to a related, but different tale in Celtic mythology. The apples Hercules was sent to get are if anything, the golden apples of the sunset.

The key to the mission, from Eurystheus' point of view, lay in the 'go' part of Hercules going to get them. The apples were sacred to the Gods, so should Hercules succeed in obtaining them, Eurystheus could do nothing with the apples but give them back. The point of the Labour was that Hercules should set off on his mission, finish up on the other side of the world, and preferably not return. A fruitless endeavour, in fact.

As usual with his later missions, Hercules started the project with a research phase. Where exactly was the land of the Hesperides? An initial false lead suggested that the Hesperides were to be found among the Hyperboreans, a people who lived among the snows of the far northern tundra. So Hercules went north, and left the usual trail of corpses in his wake. In Thessaly Hercules met the bandit Termerus who liked to kill his victims by breaking their skulls with his own, but with Hercules he went one head-butt too far.

In Macedonia Hercules met Cycnus, a son of Ares the War God. This made Cycnus a grandson of Hera, and therefore a suitable target of opportunity. The most stirring tale of the encounter is told by the poet Hesiod. [*Shield of Heracles* 57ff *passim*] By this version, Hercules and Cycnus were each in their chariots. To make things more interesting, just as Hercules had Iolaus as his charioteer, Cycnus was accompanied by his daddy, Ares himself.

Like the flames of a roaring fire, so shone their armour as the two stood in their chariot. The hooves of their swift horses pounded the earth and as they pawed it with their hoofs, dust rose like smoke about them ... And Cycnus rejoiced, for he intended to slay with his sword the warlike son of Zeus together with his charioteer, and to take as his prize their splendid armour. ... What mortals would dare such a face to face encounter except Heracles and famous Iolaus?

Then [many digressions and verses later] *grey-eyed Athena approached them with words of encouragement. 'Hail! ... Zeus, King of the Gods grants that you may slay Cycnus and strip him of his armour* [this was quite a concession, for being a child of Ares, Cycnus was Zeus' grandson too]. *But take note, mightiest of warriors. When you have taken the sweet life of Cycnus, do not take his armour too. Leave man and armour and instead keep an eye on man-killing Ares. If he attacks, for all his cleverly-wrought shield he is vulnerable. Stab low ...'.*

To put Cycnus in the wrong Hercules wanted to at least seem to give peace a chance. Politely he asked Ares and son to get out of his way, knowing full well that no self-respecting God would yield the right of way to a mortal.

'Cycnus, good sir! Do tell why you run your swift horses at us. We are men tired by labour and pain. Please, give way. Steer your swift chariot aside from the road ... .' So said he. But Cycnus the strong spearman deigned not to obey and pull up the horses that drew his chariot.

Straight away from their well-built chariots both leaped to the ground, the son of Zeus and the son of the Lord of War. ... As when rocks spring loose from the high peak of a great mountain, and fall on one another, and the tall oaks and pines and deep-rooted poplars are broken by them as they tumble swiftly down to the plain; so did the pair fall on one another. ... As two lions on either side of a slain deer spring at one another in fury, with fearsome snarls and clashing fangs; as above a high mountain rock vultures scream loud and fight with hooked talon and beak over a mountain goat ... so with a mighty shout did the pair rush together.

Then Cycnus, eager to kill the son of almighty Zeus, struck upon his shield with a brazen spear, but did not break the bronze; and the gift of the God saved his foe. But the son of Amphitryon, mighty Heracles, with his long spear struck Cycnus violently in the neck beneath the chin, where it was unguarded between helm and shield. And the deadly spear cut through the two sinews; for the hero's full strength lighted on his foe. And Cycnus fell as an oak falls or a lofty pine that is stricken by the lurid thunderbolt of Zeus; even so he fell, and his armour adorned with bronze clashed about him.

Then the stout-hearted son of Zeus let Cycnus lie and prepared for the onset of man-slaying Ares. Savage was his glare, like the lion who chances upon a kill from which he takes the life with all speed, eagerly ripping the hide apart with his strong claws. Dark is his rage-filled heart and so fierce his eyes ... that no one dares to approach or challenge him to battle. Just so, the son of Amphitryon, still full of fight, stood eagerly with a courageous heart to face Ares. Ares came on, driven by grief in his heart; and they leapt at each other with a roar.

But Athena the daughter of Zeus, wearer of the dark aegis, stepped between *them. With an angry frown she threw these words at Ares; 'Ares, stay your unconquerable hand and control your wrath. It is not for you now to kill bold Heracles, the son of Zeus. Nor shall you strip off his armour, for you shall not defy me and keep fighting.'*

So spoke Athena, but impetuous Ares disregarded her words. Waving his spears like firebrands he rushed at Heracles with killing in mind, furious at the loss of his son. With a mighty shout he hurled a spear at that great shield, but Athena the bright-eyed reached out and turned the impact aside. Bitter with grief, Ares drew his sharp sword and leapt at Heracles. But the battle-ready son of Amphitryon shrewdly stabbed his spear into the thigh which Ares revealed beneath his richly-wrought shield, the blow tearing deep and throwing Ares flat on the ground. Then Deimos and Phobos [Panic and Dread, the children of Ares] *quickly drove to him, and lifting Ares from the wide roads of earth they straight away lashed the horses to take the chariot to high Olympus.*

By the account of Apollodorus it was not Athena but Zeus himself who halted the fight by throwing a thunderbolt which exploded on the ground between his two sons. In either case, Cycnus was dispatched and Ares returned to Olympus with another major grudge to add to the list of things he had against Hercules. Nor need we wonder at Athena's peremptory treatment of Ares in the encounter as described by Hesiod. Athena too was a war god, as her name Athena Promachos [Athena, first in the battle-line] tells us, but she was the Goddess of Tactics and Strategy. Tactics and strategy beat blind battle-fury nine times out of ten – as indeed Athena handily beat up Ares when the two came to blows on the field of Troy a generation later.

Meanwhile, the search of Hercules for the Garden of the Hesperides had taken a fortunate turn. At the river Eridanus in Illyria Hercules fell into conversation with a pair of water-nymphs. These informed him that the location of the garden was known to Nereus, the God better known today as 'the Old Man of the Sea'. 'Truthful Nereus, who never lies', Hesiod says. 'They call him the Old Gentleman because he is honourable and gentle, and ever mindful of the right.' (*Theogony* 233). Nereus was the father of the sea-nymph

Thetis, and would therefore one day be the grandfather of Achilles - assuming he survived his encounter with the ungentlemanly Hercules. The nymphs showed Hercules where Nereus was sleeping, and the hero immediately pounced on Nereus and put him in a headlock. After all, having gone spear-to-spear with mighty Ares, Hercules was not squeamish about pounding on some lesser god.

Like his close relative Proteus (from whom we today get the adjective 'protean') Nereus could change himself into many shapes and adapt to many different circumstances. A rapid and strenuous bout of shape-shifting quickly convinced Nereus that no adaptation was capable of breaking a Herculean head-lock, and he resignedly told Hercules what the hero wanted to know. The nub of the matter was that the Garden of the Hesperides lay to the west, but to get there, Hercules had first to go east, to the Caucasus Mountains, where the chained Prometheus had information which would be to Hercules' advantage.

So east Hercules went, along the way making friends and influencing people as only he could do.

He put in to Thermydrae, which is the harbour of the Lindians. There he took one of the bullocks pulling the cart of a cattleman, sacrificed the animal and feasted on the remains. The cattleman was unable to protect his property, and instead went to a mountain and cursed Heracles roundly. And to this day, when the Lindians sacrifice to Heracles, they do it with curses.
Apollodorus *Library* 2.5.11

Hercules had left Jason and his Argonauts to follow their quest for the Golden Fleece without his aid, and so he had missed this chilling sight:

As the last bays of the Euxine Sea opened up, they [the Argonauts] *glimpsed the craggy peaks of the Caucasus Mountains. There Prometheus was chained hand and foot to the unyielding rock with fetters of bronze. In the afternoon they saw the eagle that fed on his liver as it came again to dine, and heard the strident whipping of its wings. It flew against the clouds, high above the ship, yet the sails shivered to its wing beats as it flew by ... each wing rising and falling like a bank of polished oars* [on a trireme]. *After the eagle had passed, they soon heard the shriek of Prometheus in agony as the eagle tore his liver.*

The screams resounded from the mountains until eventually the flesh-devouring bird departed.
Apollonius of Rhodes *Argonautica* 2.1238ff

The eagle was, like so many of the creatures Hercules had dispatched in the past, a child of that monster-producing factory, the team of Typhon and the snake-woman Echidna. Soon after the meeting described above, the eagle was briefly reacquainted with its sibling's poison when Hercules shot it down with an arrow tipped with the Hydra venom. Thereafter, with four mighty blows of Hercules' club, Prometheus was freed. The deed was a mighty one, and worthy of its own legend. Indeed, the legend was later told by the great playwright Aeschylus in his play *Prometheus Unbound.* Unfortunately Aeschylus crafted the story so well that no-one else in antiquity was prepared to produce a lesser version. With the loss of the play by Aeschylus, this feat of Hercules survives only as a brief summary in other works.

Bereft of the tale of the actual encounter, we can only move along to the information which Prometheus passed to Hercules. Basically, this was that Eurystheus had chosen the destination well, because Hercules simply could not set foot in the Garden of the Hesperides, and even if he could, the mighty dragon Ladon would slay him the moment he got there. However, the grateful Prometheus was prepared to pass along the favour he owed Hercules to another member of the family, his brother Atlas. Atlas, by virtue of his relationship to the Hesperides (see above p.145), did have access to their garden.

Of course, Atlas was currently otherwise engaged. When Zeus led the Olympian Gods in war against his father Cronus, Atlas had fought on the losing side. While many of the defeated Titans were sent to Tartarus, Zeus found a use for mighty Atlas. Zeus was a descendant of the primordial gods Gaia (the Earth) and Uranus (the sky). The last thing he wanted was heaven and Earth getting together to breed more rivals to his newly-won power. So Atlas was ordered to stand at the end of the Earth, with the sky on his shoulders, and so keep heaven and Earth apart. The mountains where the Titan stood now bear his name; the Atlas mountains in North Africa. Beyond the Atlas mountains lies the 'Ocean of Atlas' - the Atlantic - and beneath that, the sunken 'island of Atlas' - Atlantis.

That Atlas is believed in the modern era to be holding the Earth on his shoulders is a misconception held by those who have not considered what Atlas might be standing on. In fact, the ancients believed that the heavens were spherical in shape, and classical sculptures showing Atlas supporting the heavens were later misinterpreted as Atlas bearing the Earth.

So what Hercules had to do was repeat his journey through lands just recovering from the trauma of his previous journey westward, find mighty Atlas, and persuade him to take the weight of the world from his shoulders for a while and go bobbing for apples instead. What could be easier?

RAZOR BLADES

- kitchen towel

- eletric razor
- razor + bord
- baggie bags
- hand & baby wipes (face)

- Asda
- Sweets:
- biscuits
- Amir:
- sweets
- pure food

- eggs · tea towel
- butter · placemat
- margarine
- tomato sauce

Cats:

5

- lettuce
- parsnips
- fresh chicken

- beef sausage mince
- beef steak
- steak mince

- KIDNEY BEANS (tin)
- SWEETCORN (tin)
- BUTTERBEANS (tin)
- Broccoli
- Salad

- potatoes (spinach + herbs)
- spring onion

- garlic
- ginger (1)
- IEC PEANUTS (1)
- capsicum × 2
- lettuce × 5
- peppers × 5
- Napoli × 5
- olives
- pasta

garlic

BROCOLI

2 x SPRING ONION

TOMATOS (cherry + plumb)

GREEN + RED CHILLI

Carrots (2)

ICE LETTUCE (1)

courgette x 2

leeks x 2

potatoes x 2.

mushrooms (4)

Berrys.

oranges.

yoguht x 2.

- KIDNEY BEANS. (can)
- BUTTERBEANS (can)
- Piella rice
- beef stock.
- Small red wine

- Fresh chicken
- mussels
- prawns

- RAZOR BLADES
- kitchen towl

Fish mon
. SALMON
. TUNA.
. Prawns

- Tuna & potato salad (tesco)
- prawns pie lla
- salmon + salad
- Vegtable stew

Stew
. potato. carrot
mushroom
onion. broc.leek
stock. b beans

Chapter 12

The last Labours

In sending Hercules back to the west, Eurystheus has unwittingly caused considerable vexation to scholars of myth both ancient and modern. For, after the passage of so many centuries, who can tell whether some of the incidental heroics were performed during Hercules' first excursion to Africa or on the second? For example some myths say the side trip to Egypt and the killing of King Busiris was part of this eleventh Labour and not the tenth. On the other hand the historian Herodotus, who spent some time in Egypt, flatly denies that anything of the sort took place at all. This denial gives us the most complete account what happened (or didn't happen, as the case may be.).

And the Greeks also say many other ill-considered things. For example there is that silly story which they tell about Heracles. That when he came to Egypt, the Egyptians crowned him and led him out in a procession to sacrifice him to Zeus. According to the story Heracles submitted quietly for a while, but when they got down to business at the altar, he resisted and killed them all.

As far as I can see, all this story does is show how little the Greeks know of Egyptian character and customs. As if the Egyptians would sacrifice humans when they can only sacrifice pigs, bulls and bull-calves (if they are unblemished), and geese?

Anyway Heracles was still only human, so there is no way that he could single-handedly kill so many tens of thousands.
Herodotus *History* 2.45

However, the father of history knew that Hercules had a vindictive nature, was proudly protective of his reputation, and was - in Herodotus' day - a fully fledged god. So Herodotus hastily adds at the end of his mini-rant.

In talking so much about this, may I keep the goodwill of gods and heroes!
(*ibid*)

Likewise, the freeing of Prometheus, the journey in the goblet of Helios, and many other features of the tenth Labour are sometimes freely assigned to the eleventh. Indeed, if unaware of the diabolical schemes of Eurystheus, one might suppose that Labours Ten and Eleven are different traditions of the same Labour which were only partially separated when the 'official' corpus of the Twelve Labours was assembled.

We must also note that our understanding of this most confusing of Labours is further confounded by Diodorus Siculus, one of the writers on whose reliability we have depended for much of the story so far. According to Diodorus this Labour was the twelfth rather than the eleventh, and the apples were not apples (or oranges or tomatoes) but sheep. Sheep? According to Diodorus the land of 'Hesperitis' possessed;

'...flocks of sheep which excelled in beauty and were a golden yellow in colour .
This is the reason why the poets, in speaking of these sheep as 'mela' [apples],
called them 'golden mela.'
Diodorus Siculus *History* 4.27.1

Diodorus then goes into an involved story of how the daughters of Atlas were desired by King Busiris of Egypt, who sent pirates to kidnap the maidens, and how Hercules got involved and rescued them. This version by Diodorus says that the 'Labour' was not assigned by Eurystheus, and does not actually include apples, or even apple-coloured sheep. Therefore it is best ignored as one of those attempts by well-meaning scholars to 'clarify' the deeds of Hercules. As is often the case, with scholars both ancient and modern, these 'clarifications' actually result in making events more obscure.

Here, we will stick with the orthodox version of the eleventh Labour, which has Hercules again going west. Our hero had learned from experience gained in the previous Labour, and this time saved himself a hot trek through the desert. He again borrowed the goblet of his new chum Helios and took a pleasant sea cruise to his destination. This destination is wonderfully described by the poet Vergil.

Near the boundaries of Ocean lie the furthest lands of the sunset. Here most mighty Atlas turns the sphere of the heavens on his shoulders, a sphere inset with glowing stars. … Here the guardians of the temple of the Hesperides give treats to the dragon and guard the sacred tree, sprinkling honey like dew and the slumberous juice of the poppy.
Vergil *Aeneid* 4.480

According to the poet Ovid, Atlas was expecting Hercules, and had made his plans for just that eventuality. The reason that Atlas was forewarned was because Thetis, the sea nymph and later mother of Achilles, had her finger in all sorts of divine pies. After an oracular vision she had informed Atlas, ' The time will come when the golden fruit of your tree will be looted, and a son of Jupiter [Zeus] will boast of the theft'. It was precisely to ward off this pillaging son of Zeus that Atlas had made the land of the Hesperides so inaccessible, and for the same reason Ladon the dragon had been installed at the base of the tree as the guardian of last resort.

By some versions of the story, Hercules did indeed make a spirited attempt to procure the apples single-handed. In fact, Hercules made it as far as the tree and there took on the dragon Ladon. The tale of this attack on the garden was described by one of the guardian Hesperides, the nymph Aigle. To the Greeks and later followers of his adventures, Hercules is a hero who went around cleansing the world of monsters at great personal cost. However from the account of Aigle we see that, from the point of those monsters and their loved ones, Hercules was a murderous cataclysm who destroyed inoffensive creatures that were merely trying to get on quietly with their lives.

'There was a man here just yesterday, an evil man. He killed the guardian snake, stole our golden apples, and is gone. He has brought sorrow beyond words. . . this archer who slew our dragon.' Ladon had kept watch over the golden apples in the Garden of Atlas. The Hesperides had been nearby, singing a lovely song while busy at their tasks. But now the dragon, smitten by Heracles, lay by the trunk of the apple-tree, just the tip of his tail still twitching. From the head down, his dark spine seemed lifeless. The blood - poisoned by arrows from the Lernean Hydra - caused even the flies to perish in the dragon's festering wounds.
Apollonius of Rhodes *Argonautica* 4.1390

By way of compensation for his suffering, once he had fully departed from the Earth, the gods installed the dragon Ladon in the heavens. He can still be seen on a clear night, as the constellation Draco.

On his head shines not one star alone, for his brows are lit by two, and two more are in his eyes, and beneath, one star tips the lower jaw of the fearsome beast. He tilts his head, almost as though nodding to the tip of the tail of Helike, against which his jaws and right forehead almost rest. That head wheels [on the horizon] *at the limit of where the stars rise and set.*
Aratus *Phenomena* 45

Despite killing the dragon, looting the tree and making off with the apples, it appears that Hercules was unable to bear the sacred fruit from the garden which he had despoiled. For that he needed recourse to Atlas, who was able to take from the garden whatever he wished. Of course, at present Atlas was unable to move at all. But the Titan knew that in the end Hercules would have to come to him for help and he had a cunning plan suitably prepared.

Yes, indeed, Atlas told Hercules, he was more than prepared to oblige his brother Prometheus and retrieve the sacred apples from the land of the Hesperides. The problem was that he could not go to the garden or even leave the place where he was standing, on account of having to hold up the heavens with his shoulders. We can imagine that this excuse was followed by Atlas giving Hercules a long, meaningful look. As Atlas had hoped, Hercules took the hint and promptly proposed a solution. He, Hercules, would take up the load of the heavens for as long as it took Atlas to return from the Garden of the Hesperides with his apples.

This moment was captured for posterity by a carving of the temple of Zeus at Olympia, where the writer Pausanias tells us that above the temple doors we see Hercules pausing before he takes up the burden of Atlas.

Perhaps this pause allowed Hercules to review the legality of the deal he was making. After all, the Labour of the Lernean Hydra had been disqualified simply because Hercules had employed the services of an assistant.

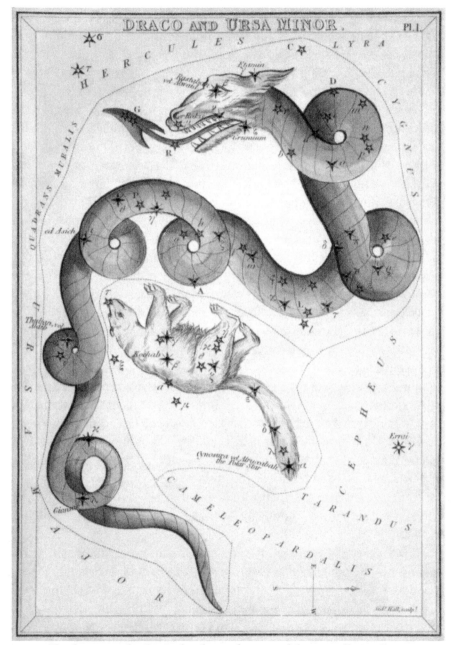

The dragon in the sky. Ladon forms the stars of the constellation Draco
Picture from the United States Library of Congress Prints and Photographs

Yet here, ten Labours later, Hercules was proposing not merely to use an assistant, but to sub-contract the completion of the entire job. How could Eurystheus not rule that such a labour was null and void, and that the count of completed Labours still stood at ten?

This is why we should accept the accounts which suggest that Hercules did in fact get to the Garden of the Hesperides, slay the dragon and take the apples. The problem was that, with the universe as it was then constituted, it was simply impossible for a mortal to remove the apples from the garden. Eurystheus might as well have demanded that Hercules make two plus two equal five, or invent a perpetual motion device. In short, requiring Hercules to personally remove the apples would violate the mission criteria for the Labours, which specified that each task could be as dangerous and as fiendishly difficult as Eurystheus desired, but not actually impossible. In killing the dragon and taking the apples, Hercules could argue that he had done all that was (super)humanly possible. However, the part that could only be done by divine entities had to be done by divine entities, and that was that.

As it was, persuading Atlas to fetch the apples was no mean feat in itself, as it meant that Hercules himself would have to bear the weight of the heavens until Atlas returned. It is fortunate for Hercules that the universe has been totally reconfigured since his day, as supporting the modern heavens would be more challenging (the planet Jupiter alone weighs just short of two trillion, trillion, trillion kilograms, give or take a few trillion kilograms.) Nevertheless, even in the days when the aether consisted mostly of air and stars the size of glow-worms, the combined weight of the heavens was enough to make even mighty Hercules sweat as he carried the load. It must have been with relief that he saw Atlas as he returned, cheerfully tossing the apples from hand to hand. We can imagine the Titan with a spring in his step as, freed from the crushing weight he had borne for so long, Atlas enjoyed his new-found freedom.

In fact, Atlas told Hercules, it was so much fun having the weight of the heavens off his shoulders that he proposed to keep it off for a while longer. He, Atlas would personally bear the apples to Eurystheus and so complete the labour on Hercules' behalf. Hercules was unimpressed by the offer, since he was well aware that Atlas was unlikely to ever return. In any case having Atlas perform a part of the Labour that Hercules was well capable of doing personally would give the nit-picking Eurystheus a perfect excuse for ruling the Labour null and void.

Nevertheless, Hercules pretended to cheerfully accept Atlas' offer. But since he would be supporting the heavens somewhat longer than he had planned, Hercules needed to pad his shoulders to soften the burden. So he casually passed the weight to Atlas while he bent to pick up the padding. It was only when the hero scooped up the apples and started to walk away that Atlas realized that he had been fooled. He was stuck under the stars once more. And there he remains to this day, by some accounts turned to stone and somewhat eroded by time. Thus, centuries later, visitors to north Africa knew that the mighty Atlas Mountains on the horizon did not just seem to reach for the heavens - they actually got there, and held them up.

We have no details of Hercules' return to Greece with the apples. We can assume that, eager to see the Labours to their conclusion, Hercules hurried home with his booty and wasted no time on incidental feats along the way. There was also the matter that the sacred apples were not intended for human possession, and Hercules would have been eager to shift that aspect of the problem on to Eurystheus as swiftly as possible.

In the event, once Eurystheus had taken possession of the apples and ruled the Labour as valid, Athena promptly relieved the king of his prize. The apples belonged in the Garden of the Hesperides, and so the Goddess took them there, restored them to their tree and thus restored the cosmic balance. Thus we see another issue which makes this eleventh Labour so confusing and unsatisfactory. Admittedly, in the run-up to the Labour Hercules had freed Prometheus from his torture. This was a definite plus, but it was not part of the actual task at hand. In the task itself, all Hercules had achieved was to persuade Atlas to get some apples which were promptly put back again afterwards. The whole thing had basically been an exercise in futility which accomplished nothing of value. One can imagine that the spirit of the slain dragon Ladon felt quite bitter about it all.

The final Labour – going to the dogs

Imagine being king of Mycenae, and *de facto* ruler of most of the Peloponnese. There are all the usual problems which face a monarch - keeping an eye on ambitious subordinates and aggressive neighbours, making sure that the peasantry pay enough tax to support an army, but not so much tax that they all starve in a bad year. Then add the problems specific to being a king in mythological Greece - monsters of all sorts roaming the countryside, and the constant worry that Zeus is about to rape your daughter. Finally add the problems specific to Eurystheus - that his rival for the throne is a mentally unstable, over-muscled individual with homicidal habits who hates him, mostly just for having been born. Add that this individual has already racked up over a dozen regicides, and has explicitly declared his intention to add Eurystheus and family to the list of corpses, and one can understand why King Eurystheus might want Hercules to go to hell.

Well, not hell as such, but Hades. Hell as a place where people are punished for sins did not exist in ancient thought, mainly because the concept of a sin (as opposed to a crime) did not exist either. Hades was simply where people went when they died, there gradually to have leached away the stains left by the passions and excesses of life. Once the balance of the soul was restored, a spirit drank of the waters of the river Lethe, forgot previous lives and was reborn on Earth.

At any given time more souls were parked in the Underworld than were living on Earth, so it might be fair to say that, rather than being a place of punishment, the Kingdom of Hades was the true home of mankind. Nevertheless, from the point of view of Eurystheus the most important things about Hades were firstly, that people who went there did not come back for a very long time, and secondly, when they did come back they had forgotten all their old grudges. A third point was that one usually had to be dead to qualify for entry, but though Eurystheus devoutly wished Hercules was indeed dead, this was not strictly compulsory.

Recently at least three living mortals had visited Hades, and one had come back to tell the tale. The returnee was Orpheus, a companion of Hercules on the *Argo* in the search for the Golden Fleece. (This must have led to some tense moments aboard ship as it will be recalled that the young Hercules had killed Linus, his music teacher, and Linus was the older brother of Orpheus.) Orpheus had been married to a woman called Eurydice and was devastated by her death. If Linus had been good with a lyre, Orpheus was beyond brilliant. He was also a superb composer and so mournful and moving were the pieces he sang in memory of his dead wife that some nymphs, touched by his song, permitted Orpheus access to the Underworld to plead with Hades for his wife. It also helped his cause that Orpheus had for a long time promoted the worship of Hecate, a fearsome but generally benevolent Goddess with strong ties to the Underworld.

Naturally, Orpheus put his plea to music and once in the Underworld, he presented his case in song to Hades and his wife Persephone. Moved by the music, and despite some bad experiences with releasing souls in the past (e.g. Sisyphus), Hades was prepared to release Eurydice to Orpheus so long as the pair walked out of the Underworld and neither looked back. Orpheus gratefully did exactly as ordered, but as soon as he returned to the land of the living, he turned. However, Eurydice had not yet completely left the land of shadows, and as soon as Orpheus turned, these shadows immediately swallowed her up again. Both had to be free of Hades before looking back, and in his hunger to be reunited with his Eurydice, Orpheus had turned too soon.

Nevertheless, Orpheus had proven the point that getting to - and more importantly, out from - the Kingdom of Hades was not impossible for a living man. Therefore Eurystheus could command Hercules to go there also. After some contemplation, Eurystheus decided that Hercules should bring back a souvenir of his visit. A suitable memento might be the triple-headed hellhound Cerberus who guarded the portals of Hades.

So, having slain all the local monsters, and after being sent on missions to the farthest corners of the world, Hercules was now ordered on this final climatic Labour, to leave the world altogether, travel to the Underworld, and return with the dread Cerberus. The Labours would be complete when Cerberus was placed, alive and well, at the feet of the judges appointed by Eurystheus.

As has often been the case during the Labours, there is some disagreement about the appearance of Hercules' quarry. It is generally agreed that Cerberus had several heads, but the number three has only become settled in recent times. Some early Greek writers felt that Cerberus had a dozen or even a hundred heads. Others give the dog a spine dotted with snake's heads and a large venomous snake for a tail, though Apollodorus prefers this tail to have been the neck and head of a dragon.

It is also worth noting that Cerberus was another of the offspring of Echidna and Typhon. Given that Hercules had already slain almost half a dozen of this brood, Eurystheus might have decided that Hercules would not be able to withstand the temptation to kill another, and so cause the Labour to fail. While Hercules might kill Cerberus of his own accord, Eurystheus was certainly not going to order Hercules to do the deed. Cerberus was no rogue such as the Nemean Lion, roaming the land and wreaking destruction. Although a monster, Cerberus held down a steady job as guardian of the exit from the Underworld. This put him under the jurisdiction of Hades, Lord of the Dead. Since Eurystheus was bound to meet with Hades sooner or later (sooner, if Hercules had his way), Eurystheus was not going to offend the God by ordering the gratuitous slaying of one of his servants. It was dangerous enough putting Cerberus in harm's way by making him the target of Hercules' final mission, though this risk was offset by the hope that Hercules might inadvertently harm Cerberus, and so suffer the terminal wrath of Hades.

Getting There

One of the first issues that Hercules had to face was that, while the Kingdom of Hades was less judgemental than the realms of the modern afterlife, it was nevertheless a dangerous place for a man with blood on his hands. Hercules needed assurances that fate would not demand vengeance for the corpses piled high on his conscience. Furthermore, on this most chancy of the Labours, the more divine protection Hercules could obtain, the more smoothly things would go.

While Hercules was a man who believed that violence solved almost everything, when necessity demanded he was nevertheless able to give a problem thoughtful contemplation. He did so now, and to a large degree, the success of his mission was due to careful preparation of the ground beforehand. In this particular case, Hercules realized that rather than his trusty olive tree club, he needed a different kind of club, namely that group of Gods willing to lend their support to his cause. Hercules also concluded that the club needed at least one more member - Persephone, part-time wife of Hades and Queen of the Dead.

The world of myth offered few opportunities for humans to meet and charm the Gods, for the immortals tended to arrange meetings only at their own convenience and for their own purposes. Fortunately, Persephone was one of the exceptions. There was one time of the year, every year, when she was met and greeted by humans. This was at the Mysteries of Eleusis, when

Persephone finished her stint as wife of Hades and returned to the upper world. There Persephone was greeted by her mother Demeter, and the earth bloomed once more after the long winter of her absence. So to meet Persephone, Hercules had only to attend the Mysteries at Eleusis, and be among those who met the Goddess on her return.

In its own way, getting into the Mysteries was in itself as much of a labour as some of Hercules' earlier achievements. No-one, even the mighty son of Zeus, could simply turn up at Eleusis and demand admittance. For a start, at this time the Mysteries were only open to a select few among the citizens of the city of Athens. (Indeed even this was a huge concession by the people of Eleusis who had formerly kept the rites to themselves. They had only expanded their audience after Eleusis had been made part of Athens by Hercules' old friend Theseus.)

Persephone, daughter of Demeter, Queen of the Underworld
Sketch from an Attic red-figure cup in the British Museum

To participate in the Mysteries, Hercules had to become one of the locals. Fortunately he had a contact of sorts, an Athenian called Pylius. If we go by a later reference this was a son of Hephaestus, and Hephaestus was a close friend of Athena. We can imagine that Hercules put his request to Athena, who asked Hephaestus, who instructed his son, for this is how things worked in the classical world. Accordingly Hercules was formally adopted as a son of Pylius. As a citizen, he was one step nearer to becoming eligible to attend the Mysteries. The next obstacle was that Hercules was impure.

The matter of butchering his wife and family could be set aside, because Hercules was in the process of purging himself of that guilt. Still, even after that huge concession there remained the charge of genocide. Hercules had personally, with malice aforethought, hunted down the race of centaurs and wiped all but a few scattered remnants from the face of the earth. For purification Hercules had to submit himself to cleansing by Eumolpus, the man who founded the line of priests whose family were still administering the rites at Eleusis almost a millennium afterwards. Only after that, with his paperwork fully in order, was Hercules admitted to the Mysteries to meet the risen Persephone.

What occurred next is unknown. The Mysteries have that name for a reason, and what happened at Eleusis stayed at Eleusis. What we do know is that once he left Eleusis, Hercules immediately and with an apparently clear conscience, made preparations to descend to the Underworld. We also know that once he got there, Persephone was his friend and advocate.

We also know that along with the task set for him by Eurystheus, Hercules had decided that his expedition to to the Underworld would also be a search-and-rescue mission.

Hercules might have expected to be made an Athenian by Theseus, his friend and the founder of the Athenian state. But Theseus was currently missing. He had gone to the Underworld, and not returned. The reason for Theseus being stuck in the underworld was due to his friendship with a despicable creature called Peirithous. The pair met while Peirithous was stealing Theseus' cattle. The two discovered that they had much in common, including that they shared a nasty misogynistic streak.

The biographer Plutarch remarks the relationships of Theseus with women 'were neither honourable in their beginnings nor fortunate in their endings'. (Plut. *Theseus* 29) Peirithous was no better. Once, when visiting Sparta, the

164

pair beheld a child dancing in the temple of Artemis. This child was later to become the beautiful Helen of Troy, but at the present time she was still too young to marry. This did not stop Peirithous and Theseus from kidnapping Helen and fleeing with her back to Attica. There the pair made an agreement that whoever did not get to take the under-age Helen as a wife would help the other get another wife, whosoever that might be. Then they tossed a coin to see who got Helen. (Actually, since currency was not yet to be invented for centuries to come, the pair must have devised another game of chance for which the myth-makers have substituted the coin.)

Theseus won, whereupon Peirithous announced the comprehensively insane idea that he wanted as his wife none other than Persephone, daughter of Demeter. Now Persephone's father was Zeus and Persephone was a Goddess in her own right. She was also, as we have seen, wife of Hades and Queen of the Underworld. Our dauntless pair of rapists imagined they could descend to the Underworld, steal the wife of the Lord of the Dead and return unscathed to the upper world - and there escape the wrath of Zeus, Hades, Demeter and Persephone herself. Such folly makes a convincing argument for the existence of powerful hallucinogenic drugs in the mythological era.

Needless to say the plan came unstuck almost immediately, not least because having decided to raid the Underworld, the adventurers promptly rushed off to do the deed without any of the careful planning and preparation which characterized the visit of Hercules. For their raid, Peirithous and Theseus followed the route of Orpheus to the Underworld, and once their presence was discovered, the two were ushered to the court of Hades and Persephone. Hades immediately grasped what the pair were planning and was grimly amused by their presumption. He pretended to prepare a feast and invited his unwelcome guests to take their places at the table. The stone chairs on which the adventurers sat themselves were no ordinary items of furniture. Once Theseus and Peirithous were comfortably in place, serpents twined over their arms and legs, holding their prey in place while the chairs drained them of all sense and memory.

To make sure that his victims never rose again from their fatal seats, Hades had the stone slowly grow into the bodies of the imprisoned men. The senseless, slowly petrifying bodies were placed near the entrance to the Underworld as a grim warning to other living humans of the perils of the place, a warning vastly more effective than a 'No Trespassing' sign.

Orpheus, Theseus and Peirithous had all visited the Underworld. None had succeeded in their intent. Now it was Hercules' turn. Those wishing to retrace the footsteps of Hercules at the start of this, his final quest, must proceed to Cape Taenaron, a scenic peninsula in southern Greece. There, just as the travel writer Pausanias wrote in the first century AD:

The promontory of Taenaron projects into the sea 150 stades [14 miles] *from Teuthrone, and the promontory includes the harbours of Achilleius and Psamathus. On the promontory is a cave-like temple. A statue of Poseidon stands in front of it.*
Pausanias *Guide to Greece* 3.25.4

A puzzled Pausanias adds, 'There is no road that leads underground through the cave,' which suggests that an explorer must have special powers or perform a particular ritual to proceed with the journey. Given the horrors that await, perhaps our casual visitor should stop at the temple, and leave the rest of the trip to Hercules.

He, at least, had no difficulty gaining access through Taenaron. From there he proceeded directly to the wide shores of the River Acheron on the border of the Underworld.

A rock like a tombstone hangs over the slow-moving shallows. The waves are sluggish, as though the dull waters are numb.

These waters are in the charge of an old man who ferries the quaking spirits of the dead. He is loathsome to behold in his foul clothes, the misshapen folds secured with a knot. Unkempt, his beard hangs down, haggard are his sunken cheeks. He does the job himself, propelling his craft with a long pole. Once he has disembarked passengers on the far bank, he returns, seeking another load of souls. But now the throng draws back as Alcides [Hercules] *demands passage. Fierce Charon demands, `Where do you think you are going so boldly? Stop right there!'*

Alcmena's son is in no mood to delay. He stuns the ferryman with his own bargepole and climbs aboard. Charon's boat can carry whole nations, but now it sinks low beneath one man. Overloaded, the boat rocks and the waters slop in from each side.
Seneca *Hercules Furens* 762ff

Once over the river things got easier, for Hercules was joined by two companions who had no problems such as those which Hercules had just forcibly overcome. One companion was Hermes. As Psychopompus, he who leads the dead to the Underworld, Hermes was a native of the place and therefore had no problems with Immigration. The other companion was Athena, who could go wherever she pleased, because, well, she was Athena. Athena advised Hercules to ignore the shades around. Most had fled at this violent stranger's arrival, but others such as the dread Medusa stood their ground. Hercules was prepared to take his sword to the Gorgon, but desisted when Hermes pointed out that Medusa was but a shade, and neither he nor Medusa could harm the other.

A shade was the remnant of a person, no more real than a shadow. However, even a shade could be temporarily reanimated. The key was blood, which briefly passed its vitality from a dying creature to a shade prepared with the proper rites. When Hercules decided that the best way to impress Hades was to sacrifice one of the God's own cattle to the deity, he either deliberately or inadvertently reanimated the shade of a muscular hero called Menotes who promptly challenged Hercules to wrestle with him. Nothing loath, our hero put his back into the fight, not least because he wished to impress Hades and Persephone. These two had also appeared, intrigued by the unusual developments in their realm.

In short order, Hercules had his man in what would have been a death-lock were it not for the fact that Menotes was already dead. At this point the bout was convincingly won, so Persephone asked the hero to release his opponent. Hercules immediately did so, and took advantage of the goodwill engendered by his immediate compliance to make his pitch for Cerberus, and incidentally for Theseus as well. Apollodorus (*Library* 3.5.12) tells us that, 'when Hercules asked Hades for Cerberus, Hades allowed him to borrow the animal but ordered that he must master it without the use of the weapons which he carried'.

First though, there was the matter of Theseus, whom Hercules also gained permission to free. Since Hercules was *en route* to the main gates of the Underworld in any case (Taenaron was something of a back door), it was not hard to locate Theseus at the entrance. With one mighty yank, Hercules pulled his friend from the chair which imprisoned him. No-one had told Hercules about the petrification process that was taking place while Theseus was seated, so Theseus lost a good part of his thighs as he was freed. In later centuries, the Greeks noted that Athenians had particularly thin thighs, and they attributed it to this moment when the city's founder, Theseus, lost a chunk of his leg.

Once Theseus was off the chair, his memory and senses returned with a rush. The second thing he did (the first presumably being to say 'Ow!') was to beg Hercules to free Peirithous as well. Obligingly, Hercules turned to the second chair, but as soon as he touched the imprisoned adventurer the earth shook violently. Hades was observing events, and though for friendship's sake he was prepared to spare the accomplice, Hades would not allow Hercules to free the would-be perpetrator of his wife's kidnapping. Hercules got the hint, and understood that there were bounds that even he could not overstep. He let Peirithous be, and so far as anyone knows, that doomed soul sits there still, forever imprisoned at the gates of the Underworld. The last sighting was by Dante around AD 1300, when on his visit to Hell he was informed by the Furies that Peirithous was by then turned completely to stone as though by the glare of Medusa. 'Thus the assault of Theseus has been avenged!' (Dante *Divine Comedy* 9.79)

We shall briefly digress to cover the later fate of Theseus. Once he returned to the land of the living, Theseus discovered that the Athenians were less than impressed by his exploits. Kidnapping twelve-year-old girls was horrible, but from the Athenian viewpoint even more horrible had been the arrival of a bad-tempered Spartan army which peremptorily demanded the girl back. With Helen's brothers at the fore, the Spartans proceeded to wreck the town until Helen was found and handed over. Consequently Theseus' stock among the Athenians had fallen so low that when he returned his indignant fellow citizens promptly threw him out again. Disgraced, Theseus later died in exile.

And so to Cerberus. The politician and philosopher Seneca has given us the best description of how Hercules seized the beast, so it is to him we now turn. We know from Apollodorus that the first thing Hercules did was to wrap the hound in his invulnerable lion-skin cloak. Since the cloak was impervious to bites from Cerberus' many heads, both serpent and canine, this allowed the hero to ingratiate himself with his target before it could rip him to bits.

Nice doggy ... Hercules charms a wary Cerberus
Detail from an archaic amphora c.500 BC attributed to the Andokides painter. Now in
the Louvre, Paris

Stroking the monster's sullen necks, he [Hercules] *binds him with chains of adamant.* [This is a pun. Adamant was any material, such as diamond which had great strength. But 'adametos' in Greek means 'untameable', so Hercules was taming Cerberus with an untameable substance.]

Forgetful of himself, the watchful guardian of the dusky realm droops his ears. Trembling and willing to be led, the dog accepts his master. With his muzzle lowered, he follows at heel, his snaky tail beating against his flanks. But when he came to Taenaron his eyes were struck by rays of unknown light. Then the conquered beast regained his spirit and shook his heavy chains in a frenzy. He bent forward, and forced his conqueror to give ground, dragging him backward as he went. Then Alcides [Hercules] *looked to the heavens for aid, and with twofold strength drew the dog along. Cerberus was insane with fury and fought fruitlessly the entire way as he was brought out onto the earth.*

But when he saw the clear light of day and viewed the open, shining sky, [his love of] *black night overcame him and he stared at the ground, clamping tight his eyes to shut out the dreadful light. Backward he turned with all his necks and his faces sought the earth as he hid his heads in the shadow of Hercules.*

Seneca *Hercules Furens* 807ff

Exactly where Hercules emerged from his subterranean mission is a matter of considerable controversy, as a number of places were keen to claim the distinction. Seneca in the quote above allows the claims of Taenaron, but the ancient cities of Hermione, Heraclea and Chaeronea also press their case, so the matter must be left unresolved. We do know that Hercules dragged his captive through the cave of Acherusia, which would be a helpful clue, if not that all the places mentioned above claim that Acherusia lay nearby. (And all might be correct, as Acherusia was the generic term for a swampy lake). Another technique which might have led an ancient detective to the true exit point of Hercules and dog would have been to follow the aconite.

This would not have been hard because *Aconitum Napellus* (aka Monk's Hood) is a showy plant that grows almost a meter tall and has glossy purple flowers that resemble the monk's hood of the plant's alias. The purple shade, and the fact that this plant thrives in damp, shadowy places are unsurprising as the original aconite grew where the saliva of Cerberus dribbled to the earth as he was carried by Hercules to Mycenae. Given its origin, no one will be surprised to learn that aconite is a neurotoxin so deadly that just cultivating the plant was enough to earn the gardener a death sentence in the later Roman empire. So by following the trail of plants and animal corpses (aconite was so frequently used to poison wolves, for example, that another name for the plant is Wolfsbane) back from Mycenae it might once have been possible to retrace the steps of Hercules to where he emerged from the Underworld. However, the plant is now widespread across Europe and central Asia and the trail of lethal flowers has become impossibly diffuse.

The myths tell us only that, Hercules presented Cerberus to Eurystheus, and then took the dog back (a relatively easy task as this did not involve actually entering the Underworld) and left it to guard the portals. We know that Cerberus was on duty a generation later when Aeneas fed him drugged honey-cakes and then slipped past him to visit the Underworld (Vergil *Aeneid* bk 6).

A few ancient vase paintings have captured the climatic moment when Hercules presented Cerberus to Eurystheus, something which Hercules seems to have insisted on doing personally. We see him restraining the three-headed beast and glaring at Eurystheus who peeps at Cerberus timidly from his buried vase, the lid of which he wears like a helmet.

And that was that. Arguably the most epic series of tasks in the history of mankind finished with a resounding anti-climax. Eurystheus grudgingly admitted that Hercules had worked off his guilt and was free to go. There was no champagne, no speeches, and no talk of a commemorative plaque. Hercules merely walked out of the palace, presumably in search of a celebratory drink. After twelve tasks that had taken over a decade in the doing, he had now to figure out what to do with the rest of his life.

Chapter 13

To bondage and back

Hercules had triumphed. Against all the odds, he had performed twelve Labours, any one of which would have defeated an army of normal mortals. In the process he had gained immortal fame, and shown the world the injustice of Hera, with whom rested the true responsibility for the deaths of his wife and children. Hercules was in the clear, both in the eyes of mankind, and, since he had worked off his guilt through the Labours, clear in the ledger of Nemesis. As a by-product of his Herculean efforts, the world was free of various noxious monsters and of several equally noxious monsters in human form. Throughout the civilized world, and in many places beyond it, Hercules was famed, feared and venerated. Our hero had accomplished his life's ambition.

Which left the huge question of what Hercules was supposed to do with the rest of his life. He was now well into middle age, and he was mindful of a prophecy that his life would end on the twelfth month of the twelfth year after the completion of his Twelfth Labour. (Sophocles *Trachiniae* 1169). Oddly enough, the prophecy claimed that Hercules would be killed not by monster or mortal man, but by someone already dead.

In the time he had remaining, Hercules wished to regain the happiness which he had enjoyed many years ago when he had combined the career of an up-and-coming hero with the role of a husband and father. Since both children and wife had perished, Hercules set out to replace what he had lost.

The habits inculcated by the Labours remained strong, so Hercules began this self-appointed task by meticulously researching his options. Among the many potential wives he discovered, one stood out from the rest. This was Iole of Euboea. Not only was Iole of noble stock, beautiful and accomplished, but Hercules knew the family. The father, Eurytus, was a minor king in the region,

172

and a descendant of Apollo. Being of the blood of the arrow-bearing God, Eurytus and his sons were skilled archers, and indeed the bow of Eurytus was a gift from his divine toxophilic ancestor. Such was the skill of Eurytus' sons that two of them - Iphytus and Clytius - had been invited to join the crew of heroes who accompanied Hercules and Jason as shipmates on the *Argo* on the quest for the Golden Fleece. As to the father, Eurytus was now aged, but many years ago he had taught archery to the young Hercules as one of the accomplished school of tutors assembled for the hero by his mother Alcmene.

To make things even better, Eurytus was evidently keen that the family talent for archery be passed down to future generations. He had publicly announced that he would give the hand of his daughter in marriage to whomever could best him and his sons in archery. So not only would Hercules please his old tutor by showing how well he had learned his art, but he would acquire former friends as family and a beautiful wife with whom he would recapture his lost happiness.

That settled, Hercules took himself to Euboea and promptly challenged Eurytus to take up his bow. After his initial burst of optimism, it would have soon become apparent to Hercules that things were not going to go as scripted in his imagination. Instead of a warm welcome into the bosom of his prospective family, Hercules was met with unease and embarrassment.

The archery contest went without a hitch, for Hercules had indeed surpassed his old master. Neither Eurytus nor his sons were any match for Hercules who won the contest hands down. The problem came when Hercules claimed his prize, and Eurytus flatly stated that Hercules could not have her. From the aged king's perspective, this was reasonable enough. He loved his daughter and was well aware of the appalling casualty rate among Hercules' nearest and dearest. Eurytus might also have recalled the fate of his fellow-tutor Linus, brained by Hercules after a dispute over his ability with a lyre. Somewhat tactlessly, Eurytus explained that he not only wanted grandchildren, but he wanted those grandchildren to survive to adulthood, and this was improbable in any household headed by Hercules.

In short, despite his divine parentage, his fame and his mighty deeds, Hercules fell short as a potential son-in-law. Until then Hercules had assumed that any family in Greece would beg him to marry into their number, and that he could pick and choose among potential spouses. Instead he was

Hercules the archer
Niobid Painter on Attic red-figure krater 550 BC. Now in the Louvre, Paris

regarded with trepidation bordering on fear. The disgrace and humiliation of this public rejection was intense and crushing. Hercules left Euboea immediately. But he never forgot Iole.

In the course of his adventures Hercules had pillaged a fair few places, including Troy, a number of Lydian kingdoms, and the lands of the luckless Augeas. Because Eurystheus had given him no chance to spend all this plunder, by the end of his labours Hercules was a very wealthy man. He had purchased himself an estate at Tiryns near his birthplace, and now he retired there to brood.

The matter might have gone no further than that, had not fate conspired to add insult to injury. Another of Hercules' old tutors got into the act. This was Autolycus. Though he had taught Hercules to wrestle, Autolycus was a son of Hermes, and like his father Autolycus was, as Shakespeare describes him, a 'snapper-up of unconsidered trifles' - in short, a thief. (His famed sneakiness was passed down to an even sneakier grandson, Odysseus, who found a way to get within the invincible walls of Troy a generation later. Also, though a series of events which we shall come to later, the bow of Eurytus ended in the hands of Odysseus after that siege.)

At time time of which we are speaking it was not the bow of Eurytus that concerned Autolycus, but the horses. Eurytus had a herd of mares that were his pride and joy. It occurred to the mischievous thief that it would be a fine caper to steal these horses from his former colleague. So shortly after Hercules had skulked out of Euboea, the mares mysteriously vanished as well.

There was an obvious suspect for the theft, and it was not Autolycus. Either by accident or deliberately, Autolycus had timed his theft so that suspicion fell on the man who had stolen the Mares of Diomedes and made off with the Golden Hind of Artemis. This prime suspect was Hercules, who had motive, means, opportunity and a record of livestock theft. By some accounts, Autolycus stirred the pot a bit more by offering the mares for sale to Hercules, who was unaware of their origins.

Horse and cattle thieving was no despicable crime in Greece. Even Hermes had once stolen the cattle of Apollo. Rather it was the sort of derring-do that heroes got up to in their spare time. However, heroes were also bound by a code of honour, and one of the rules of the code was that a hero did not steal from the host under whose roof he was staying. (Which is why Paris later sinned so egregiously when he stole the wife of Menelaus while he was the guest of Menelaus.) So while Greece was still buzzing with the news of Hercules' rejection by Eurytus, the word spread that Hercules had further stained his reputation by violating the rules of hospitality. Hercules was upset with the particular indignation of a guilty man accused of the one crime he had not actually committed.

In all of Greece, one man alone strongly argued for the innocence of Hercules. This was Iphytus, the son of Eurytus. He had been with Hercules on the *Argo*, and knew that the hero treasured his honour and reputation too greatly to sacrifice either by an underhand theft. If Hercules wanted to avenge his injured pride, he would do it a lot more openly, directly and painfully (which is why Iphytus had also argued vigorously that Eurytus should keep his promise that Iole would marry Hercules once he had won the archery competition). To prove the innocence of Hercules, Iphytus informed his father that he would go personally to Tiryns and see if the horses were in his possession. This seemed a fair enough step, but Iphytus had failed to understand how Hercules himself might perceive the matter.

Hercules was unaccustomed to having people check on him to see if he was guilty of wrongdoing, and he would have been outraged at being policed even if he was not already being falsely accused by the very people whom he felt owed him a substantial apology. So when Iphytus arrived and innocently informed Hercules that he was there to search the premises for stolen horses, he should have been warned by the hero's apparent meekness. Hercules conducted Iphytus to a tower with a view of his entire estate.

'Do you see your horses?' enquired Hercules.

Iphytus admitted that he could not.

'Look more closely', suggested Hercules and tossed Iphytus from the tower to his death.

In a way Hercules was himself responsible for what happened next. The world had moved on from the wild times of his youth. Not only was Hercules himself an agent of order, in that he had destroyed creatures of chaos and human agents of injustice, but Hercules was also an inspiration who had caused others (even his friend Theseus) to do the same. As a result Greece was now a more orderly place, and a place where neither men nor Gods no longer tolerated murder - and murder Hercules had committed, out of outraged pride and pique. Hercules himself was aware that he had over-reacted, and he desperately tried to justify his actions by claiming a return of the insanity which had gripped him when he slew his wife and children. This did not work, either in the court of public opinion, or with the ledger of Nemesis, where the debt Hercules had so recently cleared was now reinstated.

Because he had murdered Iphytus, Heracles became diseased. He took himself to Neleus at Pylos [in the southern Peloponnese] *and asked him for purification of the blood-guilt. On hearing this Neleus consulted his sons. They agreed that he should not perform the rite of purification. Only Nestor, the youngest disagreed.*
Diodorus Siculus *History* 4.31.4

Nestor, it should be noted, was another companion of Hercules on the *Argo*, and well aware that slighting Hercules was deeply unwise. Sure enough, Hercules did not take rejection lying down. He gathered an army and marched on Pylos. Since both men and Gods approved of warfare, whatever the cause, Hercules incurred no further blood-guilt when he proceeded to slay Neleus and his sons. (Nestor survived, and was approaching his 110th birthday when he joined the Greeks in besieging Troy.) The exact details of what happened to the rest of Nestor's family are unknown, since all we have is a brief comment by Nestor himself in the *Iliad*:

In former years Heracles came, and his hand was heavy upon us. All our best warriors perished. Neleus had had twelve sons, but I alone survived; the others were all killed.
Homer *Iliad* 11.690

Another son, of Neleus, Alastor, took the whole thing personally, even after death. Once in the Underworld, he went on to become the demon who avenged blood-guilt by taking it out upon the family of the murderer.

Still diseased, and still unpurified, Hercules now asked an Athenian relative of Theseus to do the deed. Since there was now an outstanding example of what happened to those who refused purification to Hercules, the hero was speedily purified forthwith. However, since it was performed under duress, the purification did not take. Hercules continued to suffer the blood-guilt of a murderer and his unspecified disease remained with him.

So Hercules went to Delphi, and there asked Apollo what he should do to be cleansed. Delphi was probably not the best choice, as the priestess there was inspired by Apollo, who was not only God of Prophesy, but also the indignant great-grandfather of the dead Iphytus. So the priestess answered Hercules 'not with oracles' (says Apollodorus); from which we can gather that Hercules was instead roundly and obscenely abused.

The exasperated Hercules was by now on the verge of completely going rogue. He decided that if he could not get purification, nor an oracle to inform him how to rid himself of the disease which quite literally plagued him, he would sack Apollo's temple, take the sacred tripod from the priestess and set up an oracle of his own.

The Delphians say that when Heracles the son of Amphitryon came to the oracle, the prophetess Xenocleia refused to give a response on the ground that he was guilty of the death of Iphytus. Whereupon Heracles took up the tripod and carried it out of the temple.
Pausanias *Guide to Greece* 10.13.8

Apollo naturally took exception to this, and the two sons of Zeus rapidly became involved in a physical punch-up in the best tradition of dysfunctional families. This incident became a favourite of sculptors and vase-painters with one such scene described by Pausanias (ibid).

Heracles and Apollo are holding on to the tripod, and are preparing to fight about it. Leto and Artemis [Apollo's mother and sister respectively] *are calming Apollo, and Athena is calming Heracles.*

In the end, as often happens with squabbles among siblings, father intervened; though fathers seldom do so by throwing a thunderbolt at the feet of their sons to separate them. Once he had everyone's attention, Zeus gave his judgement.

Olympian Zeus, father and master of us all was angered by the crime [the slaying of Iphytus], *because for once he* [Hercules] *had taken a life by trickery. If he had openly taken his revenge, Zeus would surely have pardoned*

a triumph in war. But the Gods like not sly insolence, and so he was sent into slavery.
Sophocles *Trachiniae* 260ff

The verdict surprised no-one, not even Hercules. He was guilty, and everyone knew it. Therefore it was back into bondage for him. However, in deference to Hercules' divine origins and to the fact that Eurytus had been partly responsible for provoking the hero into his fit of homicidal pique, Hercules was not handed into the custody of the grieving father. Instead, a third party got custody and Hercules was sold as the bondsman of the god Hermes.

Hermes and Hercules had become acquainted during the hero's excursion to the Underworld, for despite being the messenger of Zeus, Hermes was mainly a God of the infernal regions. His main task was to conduct the souls of the dead to the banks of the River Styx, from whence Charon undertook final delivery to the Underworld. As the Guide of Souls (Psychopompus), Hermes had little use for an over-muscled warrior with a short temper, so he traded Hercules on to a friend, that friend being Omphale of Lydia. (The profits from each sale went to Eurytus, and though the grieving father refused them, his surviving sons accepted on his behalf.)

For much of the time he [Hercules] *was captive in Lydia. He himself admits he was a bondsman. He passed a whole year, as he himself admits, as a slave to Omphale the barbarian queen.*
Sophocles *ibid.*

This punishment was meant to be humiliating, and it was. Not only was mighty Hercules ruled by a woman, but by a barbarian at that. (The kingdom of Lydia was on the southern coast of Anatolia, near the region from which later came the historian Herodotus.) Hercules did not go happily into slavery.

No man should be ashamed ... of what Zeus compels him to do. But so stung was he [Hercules] *by the shame that he swore a solemn oath that one day he in turn would enslave not only the man, but also the family of he who had brought that catastrophe upon him.*
Sophocles *ibid.*

Hercules and Omphale
Detail from a painting by Rubens in 1603 now in the Louvre, Paris

Oddly enough, it turned out that being the bondsman of Omphale suited Hercules right to the ground. The hero now had time to decompress after the stress of the Labours, and also had the excuse of compulsion for doing so. Omphale seems to have found just the right touch for keeping Hercules docile, and yet, when occasion demanded there were plenty of miscreants on whom Hercules could let off steam.

The world was running low on monsters after Hercules' previous efforts, so a gigantic snake which was wreaking havoc on the farmlands of Lydia briefly provided the only non-human diversion. However, there was Syleus, a landowner who compelled passers-by to work as slaves in his vineyard and then killed them afterwards on the pretext that their work had been unsatisfactory. Hercules arranged to be 'passing by'. When conscripted into the chain gang he promptly killed Syleus with his own hoe (and by some accounts the equally predatory daughter of Syleus as well), and then tore up the vines and set the place on fire. (Apollodorus *Library* 2.6.3).

Once word of Hercules got about, the land became remarkably peaceable. This encouraged the mountainous Itoni to launch one of their many raids on Lydia. Hercules was promptly released from his duties at the palace and put in charge of the army. It was now the turn of the Itoni to have their lands raided, and their principal city captured and pillaged. As the surviving Itoni were led away into slavery other neighbours took note, and Lydia was left untroubled for the rest of Hercules' stay.

Life at Omphale's palace passed at a placid pace. With local villains and potential invaders alike cowed into submission, the barbarian queen relaxed wearing Hercules' lion-skin robe and with Hercules' club on the couch beside her. Meanwhile Hercules himself wore Omphale's robes (presumably after drastic re-tailoring) and busied himself with spinning wool and other womanly tasks. We might assume that this role was imposed on Hercules to humiliate him further but - at least for the poet Ovid - things were somewhat more adventurous than that. He recounts a meeting of the couple with Faunus; the God who came to be equated with the goat-legged god Pan, Lord of the Forest and player of the eponymous pipes.

When Tirynthian Hercules was walking with his mistress Omphale, Faunus [Pan] saw her from a high ledge and burned with passion. 'Begone, spirits of the mountain,' he said. 'I will have her instead'.

....

Omphale found a cave with a babbling brook at the opening, and entered beneath the tufa and rock. Her servants prepared a feast while she dressed Hercules in her clothing; the translucent blouse of Gaetulian purple, and the elegant swathes that had wrapped her waist. This last was too small for his girth, so he unfastened the clasps, and his huge hands fractured the bracelets that would not otherwise fit his arms, just as his giant feet split her little shoes. She took up his club, and lion-skin pelt, and so dressed, they feasted, and afterwards fell asleep.

What will unbridled passion not dare when the midnight comes? Faunus sneaked in through the dew-filled dark, and seeing the servants passed out, he hoped the man was also. So the reckless lover sidled inwards, cautiously feeling his way with outstretched hands.

He reached the couches and groped around, feeling that things were going well. When he touched the bristling lion-skin, he yanked back his hand, as frozen by terror as a traveller whose foot touches a snake on the road.

...

The feel of the soft furnishing of the next couch deceived him, so he slipped in to lie on one side of the bed. Hard with lust, he pulled up the lower hem of the skirts, only to encounter thighs bristling with coarse, thick hair. Then the indignant hero fiercely repelled any further attempt on his virtue and tossed Faunus from the high couch.

Omphale woke at the ruckus and called for the servants to bring light. The torches showed Faunus, who lay groaning from his heavy fall, hardly able to pick himself up from the ground. Matters became clear, and Hercules burst out laughing. So did everyone else, even the Lydian lass with her lover.
Ovid *Fasti* 2.303ff

It should be noted that Ovid says this tale was told by Romans at the Saturnalia, that Roman festival when slaves became masters, men wore women's clothing and the world was generally turned upside down. Nevertheless, it is interesting that this most macho of mythological heroes turns up in a woman's dress not once but twice. (The other time was after his shipwreck on p.123.)

Still, lest there be any doubts of his masculinity, Hercules also fathered at least two children during his stay. One was off a slave girl, and the name of the child and mother are both uncertain. Then, once Omphale and Hercules had got to know each other better, Omphale also succumbed to Hercules' manly charisma. The result was a child called Tyrsenus, who later left Lydia to found the Etruscan race in Italy. (The name of modern Tuscany is ultimately derived from this child of Hercules.) By the end of his period of 'slavery' Hercules and Omphale were living as husband and wife. Another child of Hercules – either that child of the slave girl mentioned earlier, or a further son of Omphale – went on to become the ruler of Lydia in his turn, and the line continued for another twenty-two generations. Overall, the stay of Hercules with Omphale proved a much-needed break for the hero. It was a relaxed and refreshed Hercules who left Lydia and returned to wreak further mayhem in Greece.

Omphale had been the daughter of a river god, which attracted Hercules' attention to the species. He quickly became aware of Achaelous, god of the river of the same name. Achaelous was, like Hercules himself, in search of a wife. The river Achaelous empties into the Ionian sea, and is the largest river in western Greece. Its patron deity was therefore correspondingly formidable. He less courted his amoratrix than demanded her from her reluctant father. The playwright Sophocles includes in his epic play, *the Trachiniae*, the words of the unwilling fiancée.

My wooer was a river-god, Achaelous, who took three shapes as he constantly demanded that my father give me to him. He might come manifesting himself as a bull, and then in shining coils as a serpent, now with the body of a man and the face of an ox, and all the while streams of water jetted out from his shaggy beard. I dreaded being matched with such a suitor, and in my misery I prayed that I might die before being brought to his bed.

Hercules discovered that this maiden, Deianeira, was something of a chariot-driving tomboy as well as a ravishing beauty, as might be expected of a cousin to Helen of Troy. Deianeira's name translates as something like 'man-destroyer'. This title ought to have given pause to Hercules, given that prophecy gave him a limited life expectancy, but above all else, our hero was always up for a challenge. The first challenge was to dispose of the importune Achaelous, who in his own words tells the story of what happened next.

'You impose a sad duty upon me. Who likes to tell of the battles he has lost? But I'll tell the whole tale. There's less shame in losing this fight than there is glory in having fought it at all. I can take comfort in having had such a conqueror. You have probably heard that Deianeira was once the loveliest of maidens and the aspiration the many jealous suitors who hopefully entered her father's palace. I was among them. So too was Alcides. [Hercules].*'*

...

'I countered his boasts, saying 'It's no harm to me that royal Juno [Hera] *does not hate me, and that I have never been punished by having Labours imposed. Now, Alcmene's son, claim either that your parentage from Jupiter* [Zeus] *is untrue, or admit that you were born of your mother's betrayal.'*

...

'While I spoke, he scowled and, with his surging rage out of control, he snarled, 'You can win the battle of words, but my fist is stronger than my tongue, and I'll fight with that.'

'Then he came at me in a fury. All my fine words made me ashamed to back down. Tossing aside my green cloak, I took a boxer's stance and made ready, as he scooped up the dust over me, and was in turned yellowed with my golden sand. [Wrestlers did this when preparing for a bout.]

'He was at my neck, now at my shining legs, lunging and feinting everywhere in his attack. My weight was my salvation. Like a huge rock that withstands with its massive bulk the roaring crash of the waves, I stood unharmed by his assault. We parted and clashed again, both dug in and refusing to give an inch, foot to foot, fingers with fingers and brow to brow. '

'So have I seen bulls in battle for the sleekest cow in the country while the awed herd waits in fear to see who gains victory and mastery. I bent him backward and three times Alcides tried and failed to break my grip. The fourth time he broke the clinch and punched me so hard that, to tell the truth, it spun me round and let him cling to me. I seek no fame from fiction, but believe me, it was like being crushed with a mountain on my back. '

'Still, with sweating arms I broke that iron grip, but he gave me no chance to recover. He charged me as I stood gasping and forced me to the sand with a

grip around my neck.

Outfought and outmatched as a man, I turned to my magic. I changed to a long smooth snake, slid from under him and wound myself into sinuous coils.'

(This proved to be a mistake, for Hercules simply laughed at the transformation. He asked if Achaelous fancied himself more deadly than the vanquished Hydra, and then cheerfully set about strangling the snake-form.)

Achaelous takes up the tale again: *'Vanquished once more, my third shape still remained; a savage bull. Oh, yes I fought back! But he came round my left side and threw his arms around my straining neck. As I charged away, he kept pace and dragged me down. Eventually he forced my horns right into the hard ground and laid me low. '*
Ovid *Metamorphoses* 879ff

In fact, so hard did Hercules drive the bull-form of Achaelous into the ground that one horn snapped off. This horn was taken and blessed by river-nymphs who had witnessed the fight. Later adopted by Maia, the mother of the god Hermes, the broken horn became the famed 'horn of plenty', the Cornucopia. From the Cornucopia (cornu – 'horn'; copia - 'abundance') spilled a never-ending supply of fruit, vegetables and grain. This has caused some of the more sceptical historians of antiquity to consider other explanations for the legend.

Diodorus Siculus, for example, imagines that the 'snake' form represented the river in its usual sinuous transit of the Greek landscape. However, when swollen by the autumn rains, and tumbling rocks along its path, the river became a roaring bull which took a more direct and destructive path to the sea. It is quite possible that some person in pre-antiquity tamed the river by straightening out some of the curves. Even today, the curved horn of water isolated by such straightening is called 'an ox-bow lake'. The well-watered land of the fertile former flood plain would now be available for agriculture, and become, well, a veritable cornucopia.

Achaelous, father of the Cornucopia
From a floor mosaic in ancient Commagene in modern Turkey

The defeated Achaelous hid his face under the waters, but was unable to hide his shame. In later years, the mask of a bearded man with horns was a common symbol for rivers, or water in general. As for the loss of Deianeira, it appears that Achaelous soon found consolation in the arms of Terpsichore, the muse of dance. The song of the Sirens, the children of that union, has sadly deteriorated over the millennia. Where once the Sirens perched on rocks and sweetly sang sailors to their doom, the modern manifestations sit atop police cars and ambulances and their sound is avoided by all.

Chapter 14

The last years

In his final years Hercules was not idle. Though the world had run out of truly spectacular monsters for him to slay, there remained tribes of humans who attracted his ire for one reason or another. As in his earliest days when he had defended Thebes from its enemies, Hercules became a general and leader of men rather than a solo adventurer.

His new wife Deianeira tended to see her husband only in the seasonal intervals between campaigns. She complained, 'he sees our children only as the farmer sees a distant field, once at the sowing, and again at harvest' (Sophocles *Trachiniae* 30). Hercules generally fought his campaigns with an army of Arcadians who stayed with him for glory and plunder. To what extent these wars were strategic is unknown because - as with the later Trojan War - contemporary historians liked to attach dramatic personal reasons to wars which had larger geopolitical and economic causes.

Thus we see Hercules going to war with Sparta because of the death of a friend. This might seem a bit excessive, but it is more easily explained to the public than say, a dispute over harbour tax agreements.

Hippocoon exiled his brother Tyndareus [the father of the Gemini, Castor and Pollux] *from Sparta. Thereafter the sons of Hippocoon - he had twenty of these - killed Oeonus who was the son of Licymnius and a friend of Heracles.*

Angered by this, Heracles campaigned against Sparta, and after winning a mighty battle he slew every one of the sons. After taking Sparta by storm Heracles returned the kingdom to Tyndareus but since the land was now his by right of conquest, he told Tyndareus that his kingship was only to hold the land in trust for Heracles' descendants.
Diodorus Siculus *History* 4.33.5

187

There were a goodly number of descendants of Hercules around Greece, and the number increased annually; both because Deianeira was producing offspring at the rate of one a year and because Hercules constantly added to the host with extra-curricular rapes and seductions.

For example, on his way back from the Spartan campaign, Hercules slept with and impregnated the daughter of King Aleus. The indignant king attempted to drown his daughter for her unchastity, but failed and Hercules' son eventually inherited the kingdom. After Sparta, Hercules had gone on to fight Phyleus, the king of the Thesprotians. After his victory he promptly raped and impregnated the king's daughter. And so on.

This war against Phyleus was fought by Hercules on behalf of the Calydonian people. In his later years Hercules had developed a strong bond with this Arcadian tribe and was now living among them. This, despite the fact that Hercules had not earlier joined the legendary hunt for the monstrous Calydonian Boar around a decade previously. Hercules had been between Labours at the time, but had passed on the monster hunt, perhaps because every other hero of the day had piled into the event. (Including Nestor, who was then in a young man in his prime.) Any gathering of prickly and egocentric Greek heroes involved a certain amount of fall-out. The fall-out from the Calydonian hunt was especially messy, since the female hero Atalanta got the actual kill, and so greatly outraged her misogynistic companions. Perhaps the Calydonians became fond of Hercules precisely because he was not involved in the cycle of killings, feuds and minor wars which followed the hunt and were just as pesky to the Calydonians as the original boar had been.

In any case, the Phylean war which Hercules won for the Calydonians started a chain of events that eventually led to Hercules' death. Having defeated the enemy, Hercules was entertained by a Calydonian lord in a victory celebration. Since Hercules was the guest of honour, custom demanded that he be served at table by the young son of the lord himself. The boy was understandably nervous at waiting on the legendary Hercules, and this nervousness caused him to make some slip, perhaps spilling food or drink onto Hercules' lap. The irritated Hercules casually backhanded the boy, killing him instantly.

After this latest killing, the distraught hero was forced to leave Calydonia in disgrace. Collecting his wife, Hercules went into semi-voluntary exile.

Things went from bad to worse when the family reached the banks of the

Euenus river on the borders of Calydonia. There was no bridge over the river, so the family had to be ferried over. It turned out that the ferryman was a centaur called Nessus, a survivor from a massacre Hercules had perpetrated earlier. Nessus had been among those centaurs who found safety by breaking away from the fleeing herd which sought sanctuary with Cheiron (p.68) while Hercules slaughtered them *en route*.

Now one of the few surviving members of his species, Nessus hid his enmity against Hercules. He amicably enough agreed to transfer the hero's party to the opposite bank, but on condition that he took each member of the group across the river separately. This was a reasonable request, given that even the legendary ship *Argo* had complained of Hercules' weight, and Hercules had nearly sunk the ferry of the boatman Charon on the River Acheron.

Deianeira went first. As soon as Nessus had the river between himself and Hercules, the centaur dropped the pretence of helpfulness and threw himself on Deianeira. Centaurs were naturally lustful creatures, being spawned from a failed rape attempt in the first place (p.66), and Deianeira was a highly attractive woman. Furthermore, by raping Hercules' wife, Nessus would also gain a measure of revenge for the death of his kinsfolk by outraging and insulting Hercules himself. Combined, these incentives made it impossible for Nessus to repress his lust, and he promptly forced himself on the helpless Deianeira.

Even on the other side of the river Deianeira's shrieks and screams were painfully clear. Hercules quickly realized what was going on, and equally swiftly realized that Nessus had miscalculated. In the years since he had wiped out most of the race of centaurs Hercules had continued to practice archery. Indeed, he was now practically perfect.

Hercules still had a dwindling but carefully-treasured reserve of arrows dipped in the lethal poison of the Hydra. If ever a situation called for the use of one of these arrows it was now, so Hercules quickly selected a poison-tipped arrow from his stock and in a single motion, fitted, aimed and let the arrow fly. The range was extreme – indeed Nessus probably thought he was safely out of bow-shot. However, a sturdy bow powered by the extraordinary strength of an agitated Hercules could propel an arrow for an unprecedented distance, and given Hercules' well-honed skill, the arrow could also achieve that distance without sacrificing accuracy. All this Nessus realized in a single moment as Hercules' arrow took him between the shoulder-blades.

The event was captured in a famous ancient painting described by antiquity's leading art critic, Philostratus of Lemnos.

Nessus, last of the centaurs and among Hercules' final non-human victims
Detail sketched from an Attic red-figure storage vase

Do not fear the river Euenus, my son, though it rises in great waves and the water spills over its banks. It is only is a painting.

Let's look at the details and see what the painter is showing us. Do you see how the immortal Heracles grabs your attention as he wades mid-stream, his eyes flashing fire as he calculates the distance to his target? He holds the bow outstretched in his left hand with his right hand close to his chest, as though he has just let his first arrow fly. Look at the bowstring! Can't you almost hear it sing after the arrow is released?

And there, can you see the centaur in his fatal leap? This we can assume, is Nessus ... for he alone escaped of all the wicked band who attacked the hero. And now he too is dead, cut down in the very act of wronging Heracles.

Nessus carried anyone who asked across the river. When Heracles arrived with his wife and his son.... he trusted Nessus to carry over his wife ... . When the centaur he reached the opposite bank his wanton eyes saw the woman and he perpetrated his beast-like crime. ... Deianeira is painted stretching out her arms to Heracles while gripped by extreme fear, while Nessus has just been hit by the arrow and is gripped by extreme convulsions.
Philostratus *Imagines* 16 (Nessus)

As a centaur, Nessus could withstand the Hydra's poison longer than a mortal, but he knew the wound was desperate and fatal. Dying, he was no longer a threat to Deianeira, but nevertheless the actual rescue was more than somewhat delayed. After all, the river was still unfordable, and Hercules had just shot the ferryman. The hero had now to journey upstream to find another crossing-place, and then hurry back along the opposite bank to retrieve his wife. This left Nessus and Deianeira alone together.

Even while dying the centaur remained vengeful and perfidious. He pretended to repent of his attempted rape, claiming that like human males, he was naturally lustful at the time, but regretful afterwards.

The dying beast said, 'Daughter of aged Oeneus, listen to me, and you will profit from this my last ferry crossing. I will never carry any other. The blood surrounding my wound is clotted with the dark venom of the monster of Lerna, for in that blood the arrow was dipped. Take it in your hands, for in it you will find a love-philtre to capture the heart of Heracles. Thereafter, no matter whom he sees, he will never love anyone more than you.'
Sophocles *Trachiniae* 569ff

Deianeira did as instructed, and hid the mass of clotted blood in a vase amongst her baggage. Then, with the centaur dead and Hercules eventually arrived, she collapsed into the arms of her husband.

The family moved back to Trachis, and there Hercules continued his career as a Hellenistic warlord. However, the hero's dark side was again coming to the surface, as a campaign of two years later demonstrates.

Making his way through Pelasgiotis, Heracles met the king, Ormenius. Heracles desired the king's daughter Astydameia but Ormenius refused to give her to him because Heracles was already married to Deianeira, the daughter of Oeneus. Therefore Heracles went to war and captured the city of Ormenius. He killed the king who had defied him [yet another royal corpse] *and took Astydameia captive. He lay with her and made her pregnant with his son, who was called Ctesippus.*
Diodorus Siculus *History* 4.37.4

By now Hercules was approaching the end of the twelfth year after his twelfth Labour. With the end drawing nigh, he was increasingly concerned with his reputation and less with matters such as justice, fairness or even basic human decency. Also, despite having a beautiful and loving wife, a growing brood of children from numerous extra-marital liaisons, both romantic and forced, the thoughts of Hercules constantly turned to the one that got away - Iole, the daughter of Eurytus.

By refusing his suit, Eurytus had publicly shamed Hercules throughout Greece. The death of Iphytus had not - in Hercules' mind - balanced the scales, since the consequence of that death had been the hero's further humiliation as the slave of a barbarian woman. While in bondage Hercules had vowed vengeance, and now, with time running out, it was time for that revenge to be taken.

He set out for Oechalia and there he went to war against the sons of Eurytus. This was because they had refused to allow him to court Iole. With his Arcadians once again fighting beside him, he stormed the city and slaughtered the sons of Eurytus ... then with Iole as his captive, he left Euboea.
Diodorus Siculus *History* 4.37.5

Hercules did not return directly to his home, but sent ahead his prisoners, slipping Iole among them so that his wife might believe she was yet another slave-girl. However, Deianeira quickly discovered the truth from someone who had talked with Lichias, Hercules' messenger.

It was Aphrodite of all the gods who enticed him into that battle, not anger at having to work for Omphale. Lichias has left out Love's role in all this. Heracles could not make the father give the daughter to him, and slavery to Omphale was a mere pretext for his war against that city where Eurytus had his throne. So he has killed her father and destroyed her country, and now he brings Iole home. He has a plan, and it's not to acquire an extra handmaiden. Think – the man is burning with passion.
Sophocles *Trachiniae* 350ff

Matters started to move fast. Ovid takes up the tale in his *Metamorphoses*.

The loving wife believes this story. At first she is terrified of being replaced by another and she collapses in tears. Later though, she thinks, 'What's the point in tears? That adulteress will just laugh at them. But she has not yet taken my place, so there's still time to plan, to act. Should I confront him, or hold my peace? Leave the house and return to Calydonia, or if nothing else, impede this relationship by staying? ... or should I boldly cut that adulteress' throat and, with my revenge in that crime, show what a woman's grief can do?'

Her racing thoughts tried out various plans. The one that seemed preferable was to send a tunic, saturated with the blood of Nessus and so restore her husband's fading love. Unknowing of what it portended, she persuaded Lichias to take that gift to her husband.
Ovid *Metamorphoses* 8.125ff

The instructions which accompanied the gift were very precise.

I have prepared this garment for you to take back to Heracles – a gift which I have woven with my own hands. When you give it to him, tell him that no man should wear it before he does, and neither the sun or the firelight from the altar should shine on it.
... For this I have vowed, that he should stand and be seen by all, properly dressed in this robe as a new man, performing the sacrifice in new clothes.
Sophocles *ibid* 600ff

Ovid concludes

… and Lichias took it, unaware he had been entrusted with their future doom.
Ovid *ibid.*

At the time Hercules was heading homeward. He had come as far as Oeta, a
mountain range in northern Greece between Aetolia and Thessaly. The main
peak of this range is a mountain of the same name which overlooks the sea
across the narrow pass at Thermopylae. Here in later years Hercules'
descendant, King Leonidas, would heroically hold off the Persian host with his
300 Spartans.

The site seemed an appropriate one for Hercules to sacrifice to his father
Zeus, so he prepared a bull, and pulled on the tunic which Deianeira had sent
him.

He was praying at the marble altar and offering incense over the first flames.
As he poured the libation wine from the bowl the venom [in the tunic] *was*
warmed and dissolved. Released, it spread through the veins of Hercules to
every limb. Hercules resisted the power of the venom with his usual
steadfastness, but eventually his power to endure the agony was spent, and he
overturned the altar and the woodlands of Oeta resounded with his bellows.

At once, Hercules desperately tries to tear away the lethal clothing, but in
vain. It sticks to his body and takes off his skin when he tries to remove it. His
very blood is like molten metal dipped in cold water, hissing and boiling with
the virulence of the poison. Repugnant as it is to tell, where he rips away the
clothing, lacerated flesh comes with it, revealing his massive bones.

Dark sweat pours from his body, his scorched sinews crackle, and the air he
sucks into his chest feels like fire. The agony is unending. The marrow of his
bones turns to liquid as he raises his arms to heaven and cries out

….

'This I cannot fight with courage, weapons or strength. Yet while this
devouring fire in my lungs consumes my whole body, Eurystheus my enemy is
well! Who then, can believe in the Gods?'

Like a bull with a spear still embedded in his body though the hunter is long gone, Hercules in his pain roamed the heights of Oeta, roaring and groaning, overturning trees and ever attempting to rid himself of the last of that garment. Then he saw Lichias cowering under a ledge in the cliff, and his pain was concentrated into fury.

'You, Lichias gave me this deadly gift. You are the one who has killed me!' Pale and trembling with fear, Lichias tried to stammer excuses and clasp the hero's knees. But Alcides [Hercules] picked him up, whirled him around his head three or four times and shot him over the Euboean sea as though he was propelled by a siege catapult.

At so high in the air, rain freezes in the icy blasts. Water turns into snowflakes and whirling droplets become a mass of solid hail. So, as he was hurled by those strong arms, Lichias was drained of moisture and made hard as flint. Even now, a rock that has human shape rises from the depths of the Gulf of Euboea. The sailors feel that the rock knows they are there, and will not set foot upon it. They call it Lichias.
Ovid *ibid.*

The killing of Lichias seemed to compose the frantic mind of Hercules. He was already terribly injured, and it was clear to him that the poison would not complete its work until he was dead. The only thing that remained was to die properly.

There was only one way for a Greek hero to go, and that was atop a funeral pyre, and the bigger the pyre the better. Even in his dying agony Hercules remained stronger than the average team of workmen, so it was a matter of a brisk hour or so before the hero had chopped down and assembled a massive pyre from the woodlands of Oeta. While he worked Hercules issued a stream of orders. He was after all, not merely a dying hero but leader of an armed horde and also a landowner of substantial property. All his enterprises needed winding up in an orderly fashion.

So Hercules organized the disbandment of his army, and the disposal of his estate. He told his son Hyllus that he should marry Iole, that she not be left alone in the world, and gave final instructions to his wife Deianeira, the man-destroyer.

Hercules assembles his funeral pyre
By the French sculptor Coustou (1677-1746) now in the Louvre, Paris

In the event Deianeira failed to honour and obey these instructions. When she discovered that she had inadvertently killed her husband, the new widow did not take the news well.

'They say my lord is dying of the poison from my cloak. Alas! What have I done? Wicked Deianeira, why hesitate to die? Shall my lord be torn to death on the heights of Oeta, while she who did this monstrous deed remains alive? If I

196

have anything yet to do, that I might be called the wife of Hercules, my death shall prove our marriage. Oh wicked Deianeira, why hesitate to die?'
Ovid *Heroides* 9.140ff

She hanged herself.

Meanwhile Hercules had encountered a major setback in the process of dying. It was all set up, but no-one wanted to kill him. Hercules had done what he could. He had neatly stacked the logs of his massive funeral pyre. Then he had ascended it, spread out his lion-skin cloak on top and lay down, tucking his mighty club under his head for a pillow.

Everything was as it should be for a proper hero's funeral apart from two things. Firstly, greatly though he desired it, the hero was not actually dead. Secondly, none of those present wanted to be the one who actually did the deed by lighting the pyre. What should have been a moment of heroic pathos was rather spoiled by the protagonist lying upon his funeral pyre angrily haranguing the embarrassed and uncertain crowd who milled around the base, passing the fatal torch from one to the other.

Finally a shepherd called Poeas did the deed. Since this Poeas then leaves the mythological record until he reappears as King of Thessaly, he was evidently a man of unflinching ambition and determination. The grateful Hercules not only gave Poeas his blessing, but also his bow, together with the arrows and quiver.

This bow went on to have a storied history of its own. It was the bow which Apollo had formerly given to Eurytus, the father of Iole. Eurytus' son Iphytus had taken the bow with him on his ill-fated fact-finding mission to determine if Hercules was guilty of horse-thieving. Perhaps he intended the bow to be a peace-offering if it turned out that Hercules was innocent after all.

In any case, Hercules had kept the bow and he now passed it on to Poeas. In the following generation a prophecy decreed that Troy would not fall and the Greeks would never retrieve Helen unless the bow of Hercules was at the siege. Accordingly Odysseus set off to get the bow and returned with it and its current wielder, Philocrates, the son of Poeas. Philocrates had not just the bow but also the quiver and its stock of poisoned arrows. Before he died, Philocrates had the satisfaction of taking out Paris, the adulterer who started the war and who had killed mighty Achilles. (There is much more to the story than this brutally truncated version, but we are already digressing.)

The bow then came into the possession of Odysseus who sent it home for safe-keeping. That bow was still at home when Odysseus returned from his decade-long Odyssey to find the house infested with suitors for the hand of his beleaguered wife Penelope. In its final recorded appearance in the annals of myth the bow of Hercules was used one last time:

Penelope went to the hall where the suitors were gathered, carrying the bow and the quiver full of deadly arrows. ... 'Listen you suitors, who are abusing my hospitality ... this is the bow of Odysseus. Whosoever can string it and shoot an arrow through these twelve axes, for him I will leave the house of my lawful husband and follow. ...'.
Homer *Odyssey* 21.154ff

When all the suitors had tried and failed to master the challenge, Odysseus picked up the bow of Hercules and 'strung it as easily as a bard puts a new string on his lyre' and turned the arrows upon the suitors. Several blood-drenched verses later see Odysseus 'among the corpses, splattered all over with blood and filth. As a lion that has just been devouring an ox is a fearsome sight, smeared with blood over chest and head, even so stood Odysseus, smeared from head to foot with blood.' (ibid)

And what of Hercules himself? He made no sound as the flames engulfed him, and his followers stood in vigil as they waited through the evening for the blazing funeral pyre to subside. Eventually the embers had cooled sufficiently. Then Iolaus, Hercules' faithful charioteer for two decades, took upon himself the task of sorting through the ashes for the hero's bones. Amazingly, there were no bones to be found. Hercules had not died in the fire. In fact, he had not died at all.

198

Chapter 15

Life after 'death' – Hercules the God

Unconcerned, he despised the fierce flames, even as crackling loudly, they spread across [the pyre] and licked at his body.

The gods were fearful ... but Jupiter [Zeus] understood how they felt. With a glad heart he told them

'Fellow Gods, I'm pleased to see how you fear for him. I am heartily pleased to be called the lord and father of such considerate beings, and to know that my child also enjoys your favour and protection. Though you salute his mighty deeds, you also compliment me, his father. But banish needless fear from your loyal hearts.

Ignore that pyre on Oeta. He has beaten everything else, so see now how he defeats the flames as well. He shall give to the fires of Vulcan [Hephaestus] that mortal part he owes to his mother Alcmene, but that part he has from me is immortal and eternal; that part no fire can destroy. It has done now with the earth and I accept it into my celestial kingdom.

May that acceptance please you all. If anyone - anyone at all - is unhappy with this [I'm looking at you, Hera], know that he has earned his deification by his deeds. Such a person may not approve this gift, but must accept, however unwillingly, that it has been given.'

So Mulciber [Hephaestus] took whatever his flames could consume. No part of Hercules that had come from his mother remained, but only his inheritance from his father. As the gleaming scales of a snake are renewed as it sloughs off its older self with its skin, so the Tirynthian hero shed his mortal body.

Now only the better part remained in its high majesty – greater and more sacred. The all-powerful Father of the Gods snatched him up in his four-horse chariot, taking him through the insubstantial clouds to his home amid the shining stars.

Ovid *Metamorphoses* 9.250ff

Once Hercules had been purged of the remains of his mortal mother, the divine son of Zeus was more acceptable to Hera. Indeed, as Zeus had made very clear, Hercules was going to be a fixture on Olympus whether Hera liked it or not, so the only question was whether or not the Queen of the Gods was going to give in with good grace.

In fact Hera chose to go one step further. Since nothing remained of Hercules' mortal mother Alcmene, Hercules the God was now technically motherless. So Hera adopted him, thus transforming the annoying hero born of adultery into the legitimate and divine son of herself and Zeus, her husband.

They say the adoption was done in the following way – even as the barbarians do today when they want to adopt a son. Hera lay upon a bed and held Heracles close against her. Then she let him drop through her robes to the ground. In this way the ceremony followed the form of an actual birth.
Diodorus Siculus *History* 36.4.39

From there all that remained to integrate Hercules into his divine family was to find him a nice godly girl to marry. (Having inadvertently assassinated her husband and subsequently killed herself Deianeira counted as divorced.) The maid chosen as the hero's new bride was Hebe, Goddess of Youth. Hebe had originally been cup-bearer to Zeus until she was supplanted in that role by Ganymede. She was also the daughter of Zeus, and thus Hercules' half-sister, but it might have been tactless to mention this uncomfortably close kinship to Zeus, who was married to his full sister, Hera.

Some felt that the mighty deeds of Hercules entitled him to the status of a full Olympian God. However, the number of Olympians was limited to the sacred number of twelve, and in a rare moment of diplomacy Hercules declined to take an honour that would have first to be stripped from someone else. (Dionysus, the God of Wine was less bashful. He bumped Hestia, Goddess of the Home, off the Olympian high table when his time came to be made divine.)

The last we hear of Hercules the God comes from the Roman writer Seneca the Elder who commented (satirically) on the senate's decision to declare the recently deceased emperor Claudius to be a God. On Olympus Claudius is portrayed as trying to ingratiate himself with Hercules.

It was my hope that you, Hercules, the bravest of all Gods, would be my advocate to the others if I needed someone to vouch for me. Don't you remember that it was I who sat as a judge hearing cases before your temple in July and August? You know how I suffered there for days on end. You think yourself strong, who cleaned out the Augean stables. But if you'd been in my circumstances, you would admit that it was I who had the more crap to deal with.

Seneca *Apocolocyntosis 7*

How this appeal went down is unknown, as Seneca's text has a *lacuna* (a missing section) at this point. Despite this we can see that the other Gods valued Hercules' opinion and consulted him on some issues. At least as far as the Romans were concerned, Hercules had become an integrated and respected member of the divine community. Therefore as far as the story of Hercules himself goes, it appears that after all his sufferings and travails he really did live happily forever after.

Not the rage of the people ... nor the frown of a threatening tyrant can shake the fixed purpose of the righteous man who is determined and resolute ... the ruins of a fallen world might strike but leave such a man unmoved. Having such a character ... wandering Hercules stormed the starry citadels, and there he quaffs their nectar.

Horace *Odes* 3.1ff

Legacy. Part I: The Heracleidae

Though Hercules was gone, both myth and early Greece had still to cope with the legacy of the mighty hero. More particularly, Greece had to work out what to do with the Heracleidae, the sons of Hercules. Like Hercules, these children claimed descent from Perseus and this, together with their divine grandfather Zeus and their father's habit of raping or seducing princesses, gave the Heracleidae a decent claim to most kingdoms on the Greek peninsula.

The main obstacle to these claims was King Eurystheus. Hercules' old rival was still in power, and he had no intention of sharing any of it with his late rival's offspring.

It's these, the children, whom he wants to kill. When noble sons are born and the young men later remember who wronged their father, that scares their enemies. That is the first thing on his mind.
Euripides *Heracleidae* 465ff

Eurystheus accordingly launched a purge to kill off Hercules' entire brood. Many of the children were of a tender age, and they fled to their grandmother, Alcmene, for shelter. The mother of Hercules took these children with her from Tiryns where she had been staying, and sought protection in Athens, claiming that the ties of friendship which had once bound Theseus and Hercules now should extend to the city and Hercules' descendants.

Eurystheus sent a herald to demand the surrender of the children, and threatened Athens with war if the citizens did not comply. On being rejected by the Athenians, the herald retorted:

Very well, I'm leaving. A man alone can only put up a feeble fight. But I'll be back. With me will come a mighty Argive army of spearmen, every one clad in the bronze of Ares. Right at your borders, at Megara wait ten thousand men, commanded by King Eurystheus himself. They have been waiting to see how things turned out, and now you will see them descend, shining and strong, on your people, your land and your harvest.
Euripides *Heracleidae* 275ff

According to Euripides - who is occasionally guilty of taking liberties with the traditional version of legends - the Athenians were reinforced by allies who joined the Athenian forces just before the battle to repel the invading Argives. Hyllus, the son of Hercules who had been present at the hero's death, challenged Eurystheus to a winner-takes-all single combat, which Eurystheus wisely declined. Not that it made a great deal of difference anyway, since in the battle the Argive army was roundly defeated and Eurystheus was either captured or killed, depending on whether you believe Euripides or everyone else.

In the version of the story in which Eurystheus was captured, the capture was effected by the aged hero Iolaus, who had shared many an adventure in Hercules' company. The youthful energy and strength needed to chase down

Hercules and son- this is Telephus whom Hercules later saved while in divine form
Roman copy in the Louvre, Paris, of a Greek statue. (Picture adapted from a public
domain photograph by Marie-Lan Nguyen)

and seize the fleeing Eurystheus were granted to Iolaus (in a nice touch) by Hercules' new wife, Hebe, the Goddess of Youth. Brought before the vengeful Alcmene, Eurystheus defended his actions vigorously:

Understand this – I'm not going to try to flatter you or say anything about myself that will make people think I'm a coward. ...

Your son was my enemy. He was also a man with a noble spirit and a famous name. When he died, his children inherited his hatred for me. So what was I supposed to do? How could I keep safe myself and all that belonged to me? Should I not explore every avenue, and try my best to have them killed or banished? Put yourself in my place. When you have had such a lion for an enemy, you do not let his cubs escape.
Euripides *Heracleidae* 1002ff

The defiant speech of Eurystheus did him little good, and he was put to death, though the Athenians held back from Alcmene's vengeful demand that the corpse be thrown to the dogs. Since the death of Eurystheus left the throne to Mycenae vacant, the Heracleidae under Hyllus invaded the Peloponnese to take over the peninsula by force. Driven back by plague, the sons consulted an oracle, and were told that they must wait until 'the third crop' before they could claim their inheritance.

So, after three patient years in exile, the Heracleidae duly tried invading the Peloponnese again, and were again rebuffed. Only three generations later was the true meaning of the 'third crop' made clear, when, eighty years after the Trojan War, the third generation of the Heracleidae descended on the Peloponnese and made it their own.

More than one historian has noted that the timing of the invasion co-incides with the archaeological record for the 'Dorian invasion' when a tribe from the north destroyed the last remnants of the Mycenaean culture and settled in southern Greece. If these were indeed the sons of Hercules, this represents the final triumph of the dynasty of Perseus over the children of Pelops, and neatly brings the entire saga of Hercules to an end.

Legacy, Part II

Some talk of Alexander, and some of Hercules
Of Hector and Lysander, and such great names as these.
'The British Grenadiers' (marching tune of several regiments 1750-today)

No other name in ancient myth is quite as well known as that of Hercules. Helen of Troy comes close, but Hercules can claim an opera (by Handel), numerous cinematic appearances, two in 2014 alone, a Walt Disney movie and nine (and counting) TV series of his own.

In more static visual treats, artists ancient and modern have relentlessly portrayed the life of Hercules almost moment-by-moment. Almost every incident described in these chapters has been depicted in painting, on vases or in sculpture and often in all three media. The Renaissance produced a fine crop of Herculae, generally in the company of fleshy and under-clad women only slightly less terrifying than the hero's monstrous opponents.

In literature the first surviving stories of Hercules come from Homer and Hesiod, both of whom have been quoted in this book. An astounding number of poems have been written since, and there are now so many amateur outpourings that 'Hercules poems' form a minor genre of their own on the internet. However, despite the number of works which ancient writers dedicated to the hero, in modern years no great work of literature has been written to rival the 'Hercules' of Euripides or Seneca.

Instead, the name has also been used for a wide assortment of products. We find the Hercules bicycle at one end of the transport spectrum, and the ubiquitous military transport aircraft affectionately known as 'the Herk' at the other, with various boats, trains and aeroplanes in between. You could even once buy the Hercules version of an old Model T Ford.

You will find Hercules in ageing computers (thanks to a once-popular graphics card) and in the latest models, thanks to an ARM processor. Hercules is in California, as a mighty sequoia tree, and, in the same state, the town of Hercules joins older places such as Eraclea in Italy and at least eight cities in in the ancient world named after the hero. Hercules would also have loved being the namesake of Hercules the Liger, who at 3.3 meters and 418kg makes the Nemean Lion look like a kitty.

Hercules is certainly in the heavens, not only because myth has placed him there, but because NASA has done so too with a satellite project. Also, there is not only a Hercules constellation, but Hercules being Hercules, our hero goes over the top in the matter, so there is also the Hercules dwarf galaxy, and the Hercules super-clusters of galaxies, just one of which numbers at least 100 galaxies. Beat that, Hera.

The mighty Hercules today
Picture by USAF Tech. Sgt. Brian E. Christiansen

Why this enduring fascination with an over-muscled thug, murderer and child-killer? It cannot be merely the massive strength of Hercules, because fiction could easily have invented characters both stronger and more noble. In fact both fiction and legend have tried, but only Superman has survived. (Spawning, inevitably, both 'Superman versus Hercules' comic books and internet debate as to who is stronger.)

However, Hercules is much more than a set of muscles. He is a person. Not a very likeable person, but a very real human with a force of personality so strong that it remained consistent through a thousand years of ancient literature and in the different cultures of Greece and Rome.

Hercules is prickly and proud, not very articulate and always ready to fall back on his core strength, which is, well, his strength. He is inconsiderate,

206

wilful and impulsive. He will happily bite something off first and see if he can chew it afterwards. Whether he is right or wrong he is never uncertain. He anguishes over his past and can get gloomy about his future, but actual fear is unknown to him.

Hercules has an elastic code of honour which, to be fair, was shared by his contemporaries and even his gods. With Hercules that code stretches to include rape, murder and robbery, but by the standards of his day Hercules seldom stretched that code past breaking point. Hercules considered himself an honourable man, and the fact that he would brain you for disagreeing with him was quite consistent with his personal standards.

Hercules is not malicious. While ruthless in pursuit of his objectives, he never inflicts pain or humiliation simply for the sake of it. On occasion he goes out of his way to help others with no immediate prospect of being rewarded for doing so. Finally, he is intelligent. We see Hercules starting each of his labours with careful research and planning, and from the beginning he was a good general and leader of men. He was, after all, a protégé of Athena, the Goddess of Rationality.

In short, Hercules was no squeaky-clean hero with gleaming teeth and a chiselled chin. Modern attempts to portray him in this way do his legend no favours. Hercules was human, and a deeply flawed human at that. He achieved his heroic feats not because of who he was, but despite who he was. The challenge which Hercules faced is still us with each of us today - to wrestle with our limitations and the monsters within us, to overcome our flaws and failings and then, like Hercules, to go on and become something extraordinary.

Bibliography

Modern Works

There is a huge corpus of scholarly and popular texts on Hercules. The following are those most used in the preparation of this book. The Eidinow & Kindt book is included as recommended reading.

Allen, T. *A Hand-Book of Classical Geography, Chronology, Mythology, and Antiquities*, Forgotten Books: Classic Reprint, 2012

Blanshard, A. *Hercules: A Heroic Life*, Granta Books, 2005

Campbell, J. *The Power of Myth*, Anchor, 1991

Edmunds, L. (ed) *Approaches to Greek Myth* (2nd edition), Johns Hopkins University Press, 2014

Eidinow, E. & Kindt, J. (eds) *The Oxford Handbook of Ancient Greek Religion* 1st Edition, Oxford Handbooks in Classics and Ancient History, Oxford University Press, 2015

Eisner, R. 'Euripides' Use of Myth', *Arethusa* 12.2, p.153ff.,1979

Fuqua, C. 'Heroism, Heracles, and the 'Trachiniae', *Traditio* Vol. 36 , pp. 1-81, 1980

Hornblower S. & Spawforth A. (eds) *The Oxford Classical Dictionary*, Oxford University Press. 2012

Kirk G. 'The Mythical Life of Heracles', *The Nature of Greek Myths*, Harmondsworth, 1974

Matyszak, P. *The Greek and Roman Myths*, Thames and Hudson, 2010

Padilla, M. *The Myths of Herakles in Ancient Greece: Survey and Profile*, University Press of America, 1998

Piggott, S. 'The Hercules Myth – Beginnings and Ends', *Antiquity* 12.47, pp 323-331, 1938.

Rawlings, L. Bowden, H. Rawlings, M. (ed.) *Herakles and Hercules*, Classical Press of Wales, 2006

Shapiro, J. *Mao's War Against Nature: Politics and the Environment in Revolutionary China*, Cambridge University Press, 2001

Ancient Texts
While I have quoted from numerous ancient sources, these are the ones I have used most extensively:

Apollodorus
  Library Book II (History)
Apollonius
  Argonautica (Epic poem)
Diodorus Siculus
  The Library of History Books IV-VI (History)
Euripides
  The Madness of Heracles (Play)
  Heraclidae (Play)
  Alcestis (Play)
Hesiod
  Theogony (Discursive poem)
  The Shield of Heracles (Epic poem)
Homer
  The Iliad (Epic Poem)
  The Odyssey (Epic poem)
  The Homeric Hymns (Religious verses attributed to Homer)
Hyginus
  Fabulae (Fables)
Ovid
  Metamorphoses (Fables)
  Fasti   (Epic poems)
  Heroides (Satire)
Pausanius
  Guide to Greece (Travel Guide)
Philostratus the Elder
  Imagines (Art Textbook)
Plautus
  Amphitryon (Play)
Quintus Smyrnaeus
  The Fall of Troy/Posthomerica (Epic poem)
Seneca the Younger

Index

Printed in Great Britain
by Amazon

83503112R00133